Data Rookies Labs: Intro to Analytics with Orange

Visual, No-Code Labs for Beginners

Data Analytics Curriculum, LLC

About the Publisher

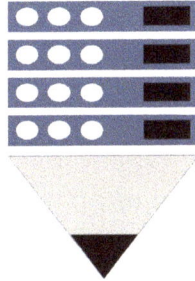

Data Analytics Curriculum

Data Analytics Curriculum, LLC creates approachable, visually engaging educational materials that make data science and ai related technology accessible for learners from high school to college and independent study.

Please see our website or TPT online store for additional titles and resources such as slides, additional book forms, content (non lab) textbooks to accompany these labs, solution guides and other resources to help you teach and learn.

Additional resources available:

Website: https://www.dataanalyticscurriculum.com

Acknowledgement

This book makes use of Orange Data Mining software, developed by the Bioinformatics Laboratory at the University of Ljubljana. Orange is open-source software released under the GNU General Public License v3.

For more information, visit https://orange.biolab.si.

All screenshots, workflows, and examples based on Orange are used in compliance with this license.

Contents

Lab 1

Get Started with Orange

Orange is a free, open-source data mining tool that uses visual programming with Python in the background. It allows you to explore data analysis workflows without writing code. It is available for download at orangedatamining.com.

Because Orange runs on Python you must first have Python installed although Orange guides you through this if it does not detect a prior installation. Orange requires no coding unless advanced usage is intended although it does fully integrate with Python and understand the language.

Note Orange does a base installation. There are additional packages available that need to be installed as add ins for specific tasks (such as Text Analytics or Association Analysis).

1.1 Lesson Steps

Step 1: Starting Orange

When you first launch Orange a Welcome Screen appears.

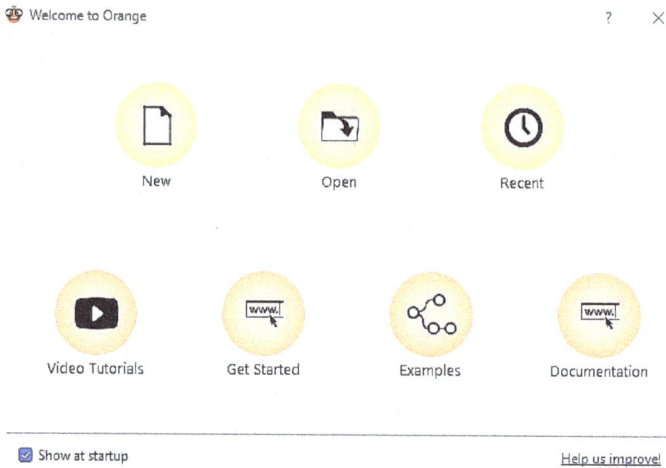

From here you have the options of starting a new workflow, opening a recent (workflow) file, or exploring documentation and tutorials Orange provides online. Select the option to start a new workflow.

Step 2: Orange Interface Overview

Let's get familiar with the Orange environment. There are two main components. On the right is the Canvas area (which is simply a blank white workspace which on start-up has nothing in it). On the left is a widget directory (the left panel). This is where you can obtain the widgets you need and drag and drop them onto the workspace. Note that the widgets are grouped by tasks (Data, Visualize, etc.).

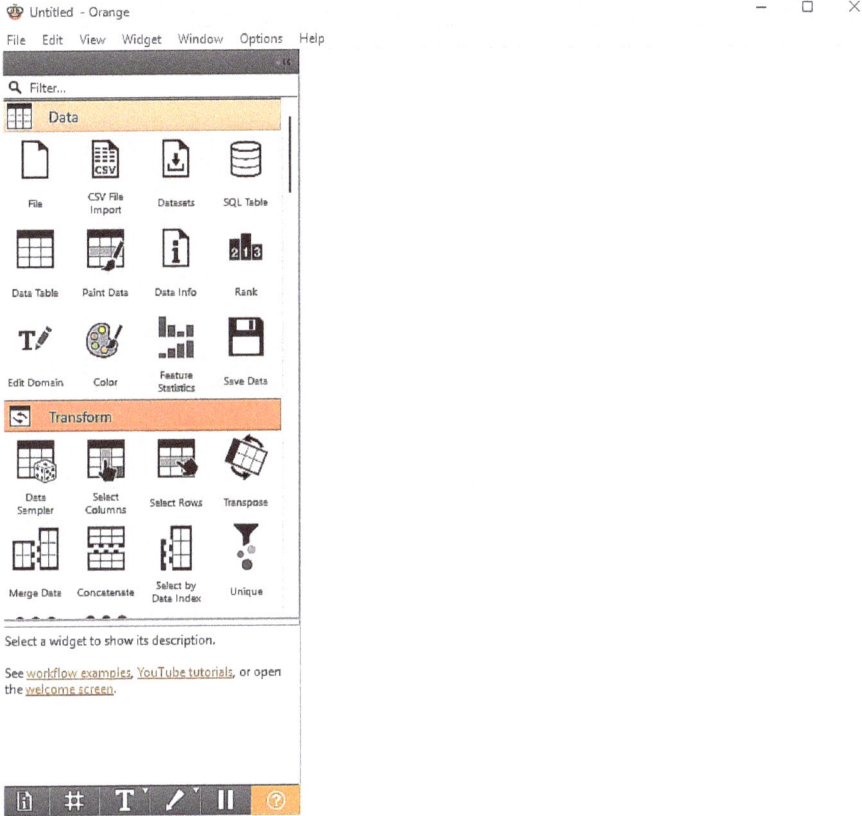

Step 3: Widgets

Widgets are modular tools for tasks like data import, analysis, and visualization. Underneath (and invisible to you) each widget is Python specific programming. When you use widgets you are effectively sending input and receiving output form the underlying Python code, but you do not need to do any coding to use Orange.

As you hover over the widgets it gives details on what each widget does (on the bottom left). Read the descriptions shown. Each widget has a specific role. For example, the File widget loads data from your computer, while Datasets can load example files. Understanding each widget's function helps you choose the right one for your task.

Step 4: Load Sample Data

Now let's create a practice workflow and get you ready to use Orange. Drag a Datasets widget from the Data group onto the Canvas.

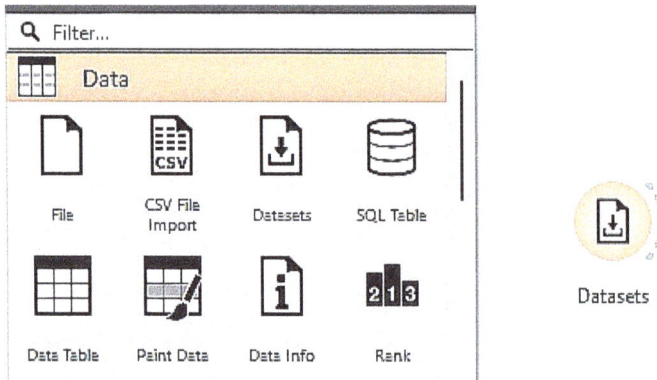

Double-click to open it and select Iris dataset which is built into the system (we are not yet loading external data).

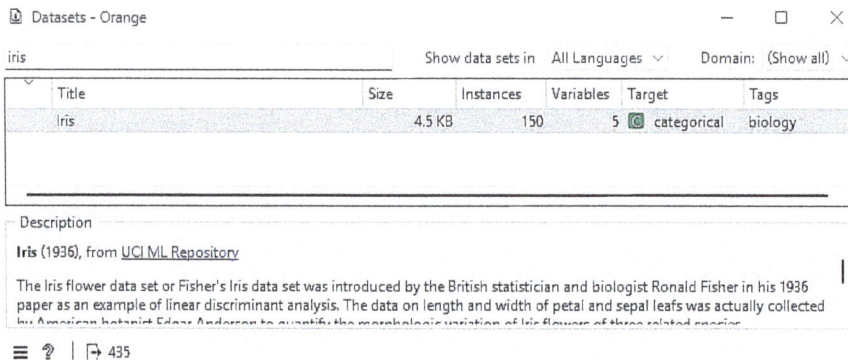

Step 5: View the Data

Add a Data Table widget to the canvas. Connect this to the Datasets widget.

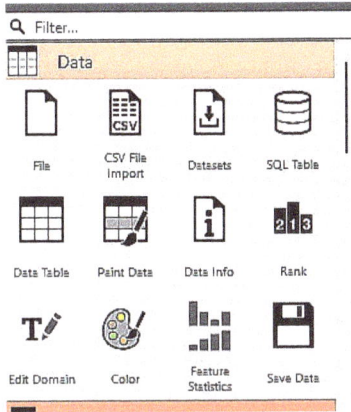

Click on the Data Table widget to view the data.

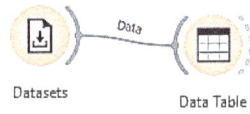

Step 6: Visualize the Data

From the Visualize group, drag a Scatter Plot widget onto the canvas. Connect the Data Table to the Scatter Plot.

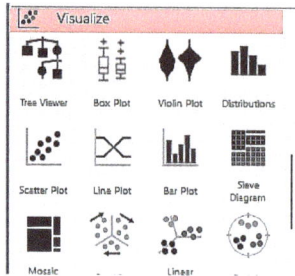

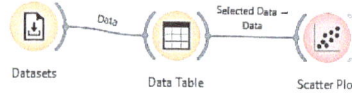

Double-click Scatter Plot to view the graph (play around with the graph axis and settings to explore more).

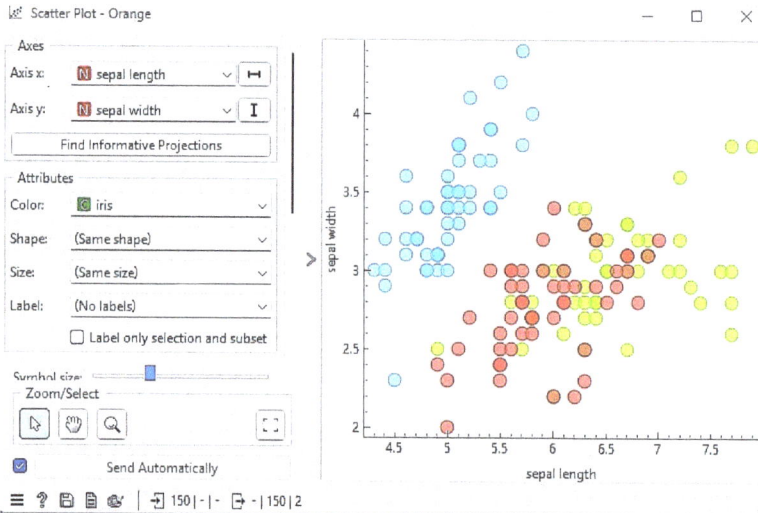

Step 7: Save Your Work

Go to File > Save As. Save the project with a name. Orange saves files as .ows (Orange Workflow Schema). You can also export results or create a journal for sharing.

Very importantly - once a workflow is setup and saved it can be used for different data simply by using a different dataset in the starting widget. This can be very helpful to not always have to start each workflow from scratch.

1.2 Wrap-Up

This lab was introduction to Orange's visual programming environment. It covered how to launch the app, add and connect widgets, load sample data, and view simple visualizations. Orange makes it simple to do analytics and you can build and reuse workflows, and you don't have to write code. Now you are ready to learn NLP.

Lab 2

Understanding Data

In this lab, you'll explore different types of data using Orange, a visual data analysis tool. With a real-world dataset about student performance, you'll get practical experience working with core data concepts in a way that's easy to follow and interpret.

This tutorial focuses on structured data—that is, data organized in rows and columns like a spreadsheet. Each column, or feature, such as "gender" or "math score," has a clear label and a specific data type. This format is common in surveys, spreadsheets, and databases. In a later lab, you'll work with unstructured data like text, images, or audio—types that don't fit neatly into tables and require different approaches to analyze.

2.1   Lesson Steps

Step 1: Load data

Open a new workflow in Orange. Add to the canvas a new File widget. Open the file widget and load the data 'Ex2_1.csv'.

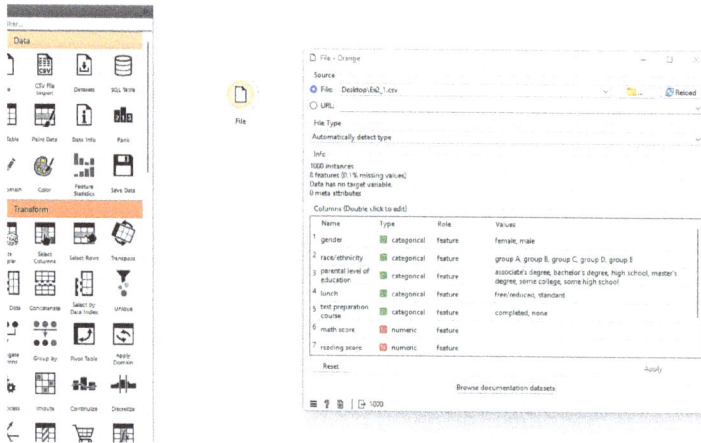

Using the File widget Orange seems to detect the correct data types (unlike the plain CSV import widget). Since CSV files don't include metadata, Orange is essentially making educated guesses when assigning types. So, you should always review the data and data types assigned after uploading.

Our sample data includes student exam results and background information. There's a mix of quantitative numeric (continuous) features like math and reading scores, and qualitative categorical ones such as gender, race/ethnicity, and lunch type.

The feature parental level of education is an example of an ordinal categorical feature, meaning it has a natural order (like high school < bachelor's < master's).

Step 2: View Data Table

Next, after the data is loaded, connect the File widget to a Data Table widget and open it.

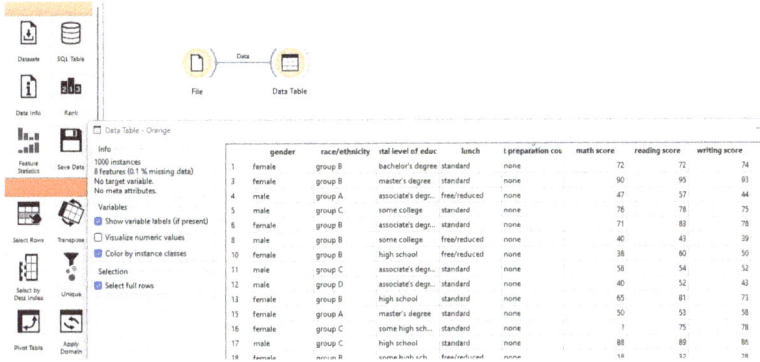

A data table is the definition of how structured data typically is organized. In this data each row represents a student, and each column is a feature such as gender, math score, or parental education.

In the data table view. Orange displays the total number of entries (for example, 1,000 students). It also shows missing data percentage. Note it specifies something called 'target' variable as well - a target variable is your 'y' variable in algebra. Often in data analysis we are doing some type of modelling with a target variable and setting these correctly in Orange is very important.

Click the option under 'Variables' on the left to visualize numeric values.

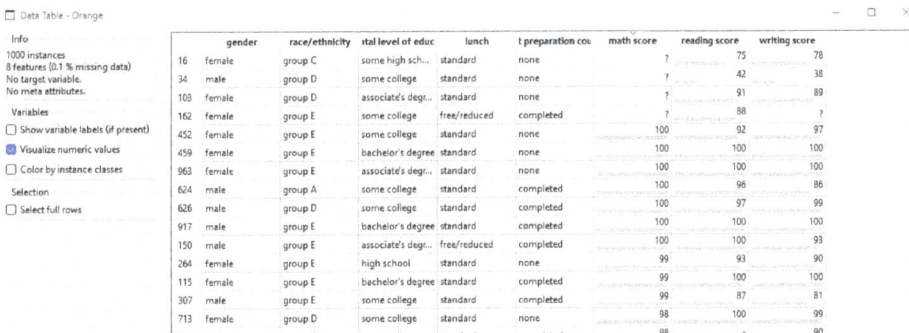

This setting adds small horizontal bars inside the numeric cells to represent value size, making it quicker to compare values and spot patterns as the bars are proportional to the data values. Try sorting the math scores by clicking the column header. You will also note there are some missing values.

Step 3: Look at Features

Each row in the table is a record, and each column is a feature, or a specific attribute of the student. Features are what is generically called variables and include things like gender, math score, or parental education.

In data science, understanding features is essential—they help describe the dataset and are used in analysis or for making predictions. Orange has a widget for quick viewing features. Add a Feature Statistics widget to your workflow by connecting it to the Data Table, then open it.

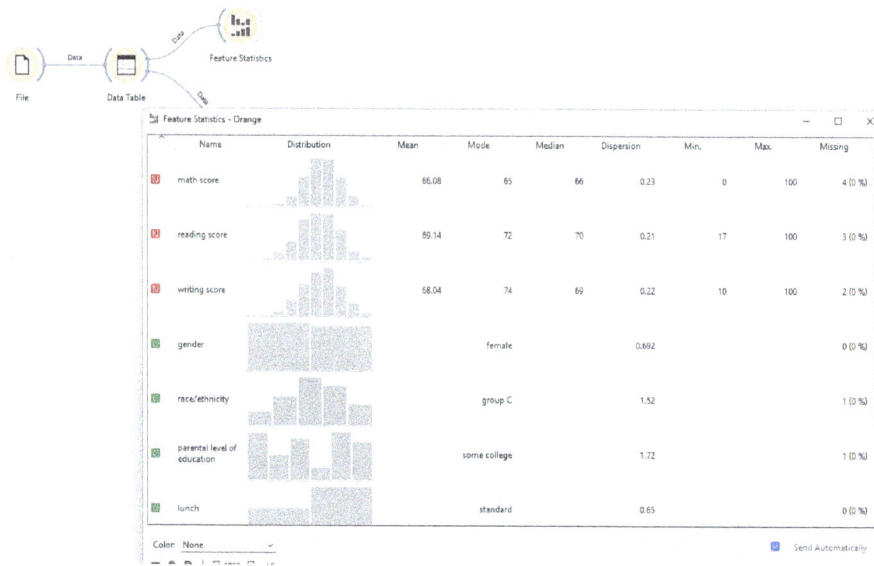

The Feature statistics widget gives a quick summary of data: how many unique values a feature has, the most frequent value, the average (for numeric fields), and any missing data. It's a good starting point for spotting unusual values or deciding how to clean or prep the data for analysis.

Step 4: Look Data Types

Since Orange tries to infer data types and can make errors (especially with CSVs), it's important to check that everything is correct and make changes if needed.

Use the Edit Domain widget is one way to do this. It allows you to adjust metadata about your features—without altering the underlying data. You can rename columns, change data types (like switching from numeric to categorical), set the role of a feature (regular, target, or meta), remove or add columns, or re-label values.

Add the Edit Domain widget to your workflow and connect it to the Data Table (not to Feature Statistics, since that widget doesn't pass data through).

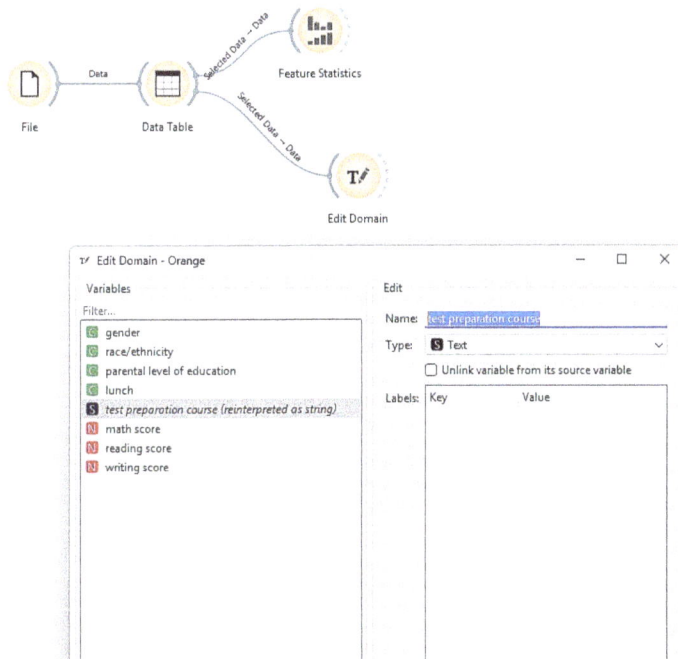

This data looks pretty good. To illustrate what can be done with this widget change the data type of variable 'test preparation course' to Text from cate-

gorical. Changing variable type makes that variable eligible for different pro-
cessing and analytical purposes. Changing a feature type to text would for
example make it eligible to use in text preprocessing but not make it eligible
to be a categorical target variable.

Step 5: Examine New Data

Connect a new Data Table widget to the Edit Domain widget and then a Select
Columns widget and open it.

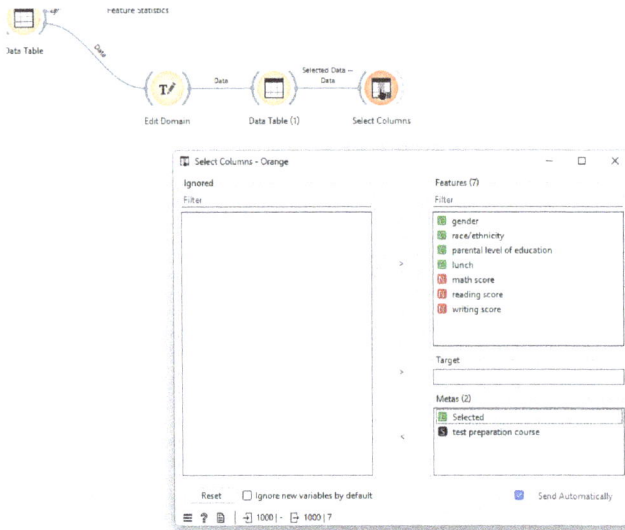

The 'test preparation course' variable is now listed as a meta variable. When
Orange detects a text feature, it automatically classifies it this way. Meta variables aren't used directly in modeling or analysis but are still available for
labeling, reference, or identifying records.

Step 6: Create New Variable

Sometimes you need a variable with a derived calculation or of a different
type based on the data. For example, you might want to convert math scores
into categories like "High" and "Low" to explore differences between groups

instead of exact numbers.

To do this add a Formula widget to the Data Table created in Step 5 (to pre-serve modifications done there we do not want to go back to the starting data), then add a Discretize widget and a new Data Table widget. Connect these as shown.

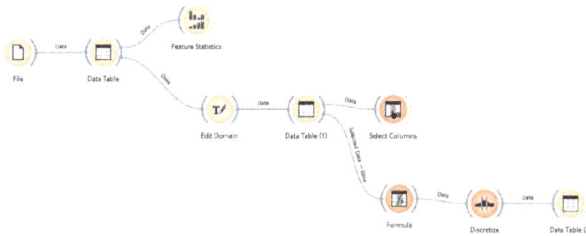

Open the formula widget, create a new variable called mathCategory and set it equal to math scores. This is simply making a duplicate variable that we can discretize to a categorical variable so that the original variable is not over-written. Click the send button on the bottom and close the Formula widget.

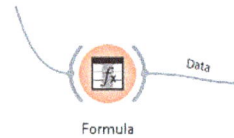

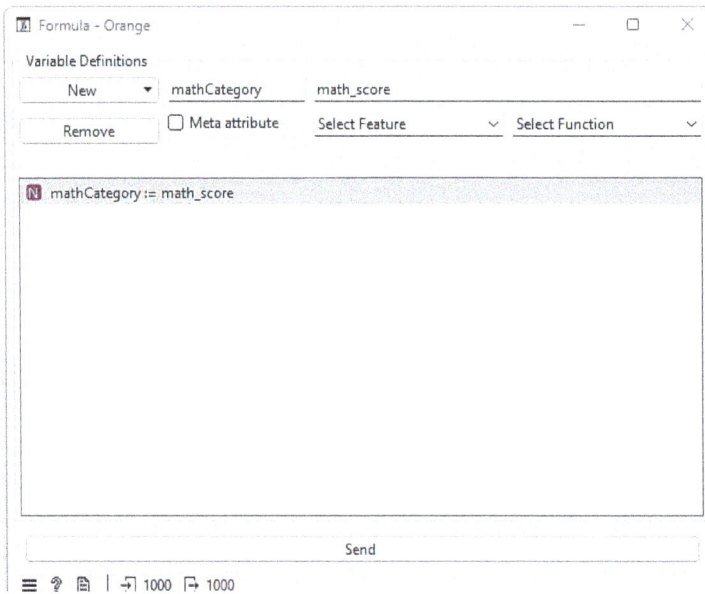

Next click on the Discretize widget, select the MathCategory variable and set custom to 0, 0.7 which dichotomizes the math scores to a variable of greater than or less than 70 (high and low scores, this could be re-labelled, but we will not so here).

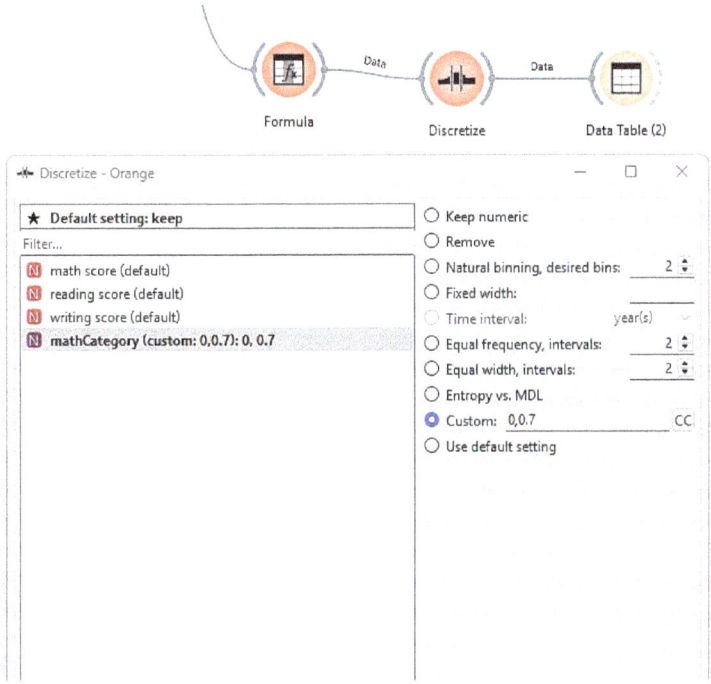

Next open the final Data Table to view.

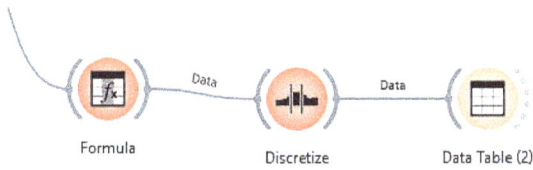

c₂	lunch	math score	reading score	writing score	mathCategory
ee	standard	72	72	74	≥ 0.7
	standard	69	90	88	≥ 0.7
	standard	90	95	93	≥ 0.7
..	free/reduced	47	57	44	≥ 0.7
	standard	76	78	75	≥ 0.7
..	standard	71	83	78	≥ 0.7
	standard	88	95	92	≥ 0.7
	free/reduced	40	43	39	≥ 0.7
	free/reduced	64	64	67	≥ 0.7

Now there is new categorical variable (the data type can be changed as well). This example would let you use high or low math scores as a categorical target variable which you could not do with the current continuous numeric form of the variable.

2.2 Wrap-Up

In this lab, you worked with structured data using a dataset on student performance. You explored the basics of loading and viewing data, checked feature types, and learned how to clean or adjust them when needed. You also practiced creating a new categorical variable from numeric data, which can be useful for grouping or classification tasks later.

These steps are an important foundation for further work.

2.3 Exercises

Understanding Data

These exercises practice what is learned by doing this lab.

Dataset 1: Employee Data
File: employee_demo.csv

This dataset contains fictional HR data, including demographic and job-related information such as department, education level, salary, years of experience, and job satisfaction.

1. How many rows (instances) and columns (features) are in this dataset?

2. Identify one numerical, one categorical, and one ordinal feature in the dataset.

3. Use the Feature Statistics widget and report on the average salary. (Paste output)

4. Which department has the most employees? Use Feature Statistics to find this. (Paste the value)

5. Use the Edit Domain widget to convert JobSatisfaction to text. What happens to its status in the next Data Table? (Answer in words)

Dataset 2: Hospital Patient Data
File: hospital_small.csv

This dataset contains information about patients, including demographic and clinical features like age, gender, diagnosis, and recovery time.

6. Which feature(s) in this dataset are suitable for discretization? Why? (Answer in words)

7. Create a new variable in Formula called RiskAge equal to Age. Then discretize it into 2 bins: under 50 and over 50. Paste a screenshot of the result in the Data Table.

8. After discretization, how many patients fall into each age group? (Paste counts or describe what you observe in Orange)

9. Use Feature Statistics to determine which diagnosis has the longest average recovery time. (Paste value or description)

10. Using the Edit Domain widget, convert Smoker to a numeric feature. What might be the advantage or disadvantage of doing this? (Answer in words)

Lab 3

Unstructured Data Basics

3.1   Lesson Steps

Step 0: Add Text Mining Menu

To add text mining in Orange, you first need to install the Text Mining add-on as it may not have been part of the default package installation. If you don't have it installed (aka: it does not appear as a menu of widgets) then go to the top menu bar in Orange. Click on Options, then choose Add-ons. From the list, find and select Text Mining, then click Install. After it finishes installing, restart Orange. Once done, the new menu of text mining widgets will appear, letting you analyze and work with text data easily.

21

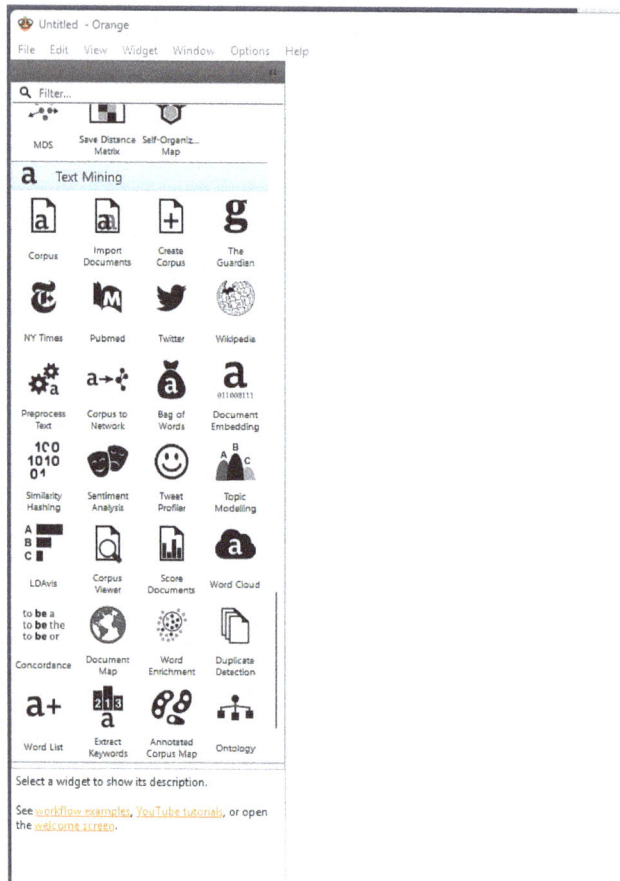

Step 1: Load Text Data (Corpus)

In text analysis, a corpus refers to a collection of documents you want to ex-plore. These might be short passages, essays, or paragraphs. Orange pro-vides a sample corpus called book-excerpts.tab, which contains short selec-tions from various books.

To begin, add the Corpus widget to the work space. Open the widget and load the book-excerpts.tab from the sample data folder (this is installed with Orange).

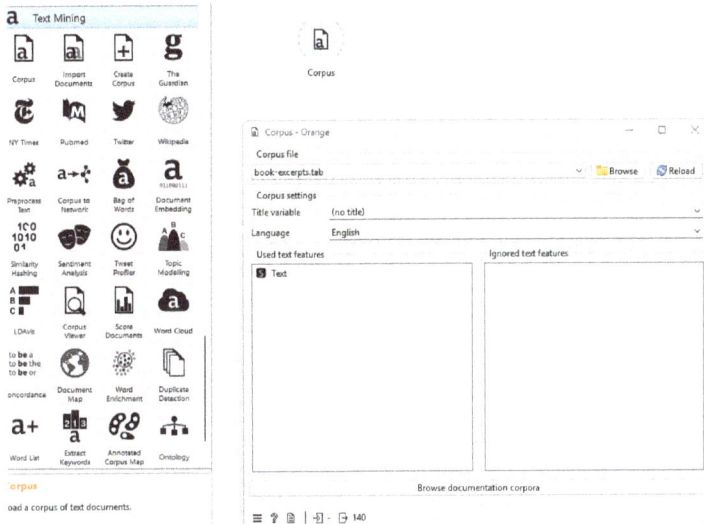

To look at the text (which unlike a data table a corpus will not let you just click and view), add a Corpus Viewer widget and connect it to the Corpus. Open the viewer to browse the contents. This gives a preview like how a Data Table works with structured data and you can see what the data is.

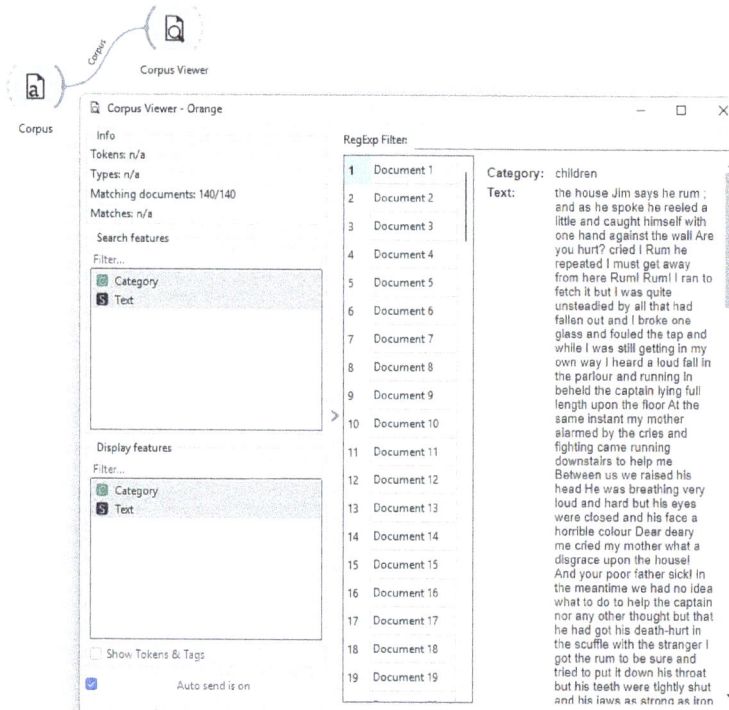

Step 2: Preprocess Text

Before analyzing the text, it needs to be converted to a workable form. This is vastly different from structured data. This process is called preprocessing. In Orange, this is done using the Preprocess Text widget, which includes several functions in one place.

Rather than running all processes at once, this lab will go step by step to better understand what each one does.

To begin preprocessing, connect the Corpus to a Preprocess Text widget. Remove any default steps already listed by clicking the small x on the right side of each one. Add Tokenize and Regexp Tokenizer from the available options. This breaks the text into individual words or tokens.

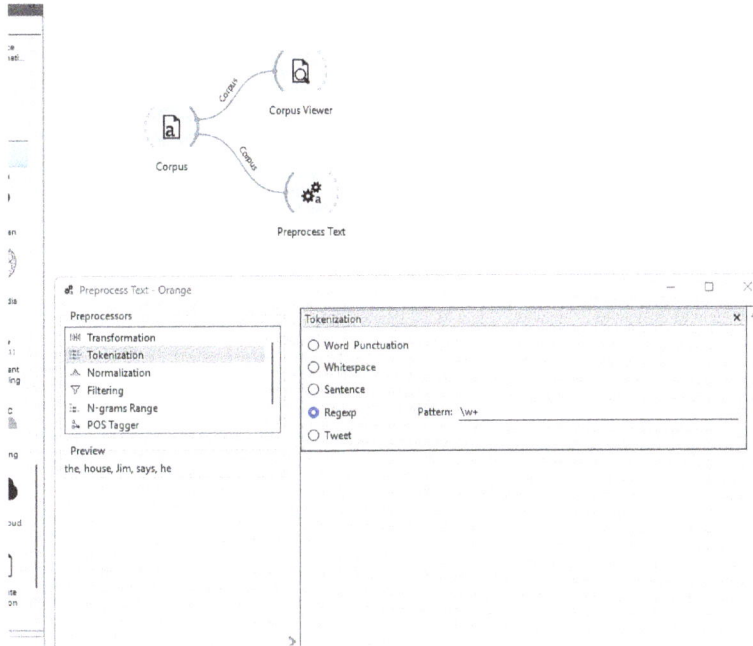

To check the result, connect a Corpus Viewer to this widget and open it. In the viewer, make sure Show Tokens and Tags is checked at the bottom left. The right side of the Corpus View has a scroll bar so you can look over your text if it is long.

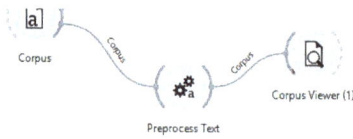

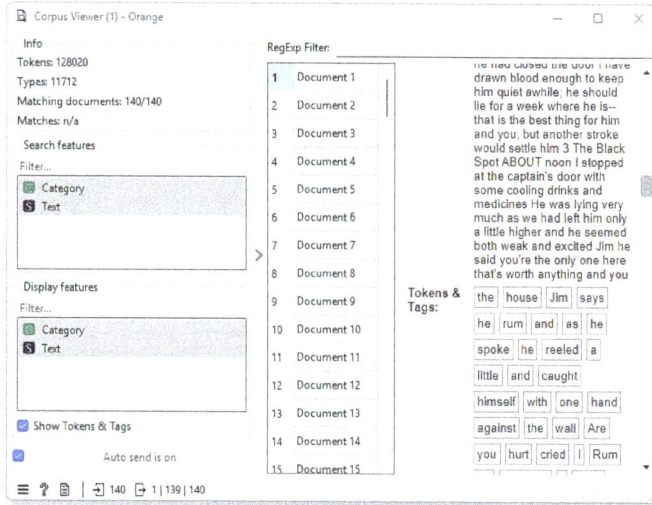

Next, connect a second Preprocess Text widget to the first. Now we will do a lowercase transformation. This step converts all words to lowercase so that variations like "Data" and "data" are treated the same (capital and small letters are coded differently in computers and have different character value identifiers). Open the widget, select Transformation Lowercase, and remove all other options.

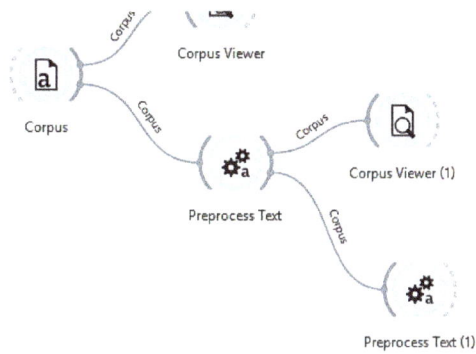

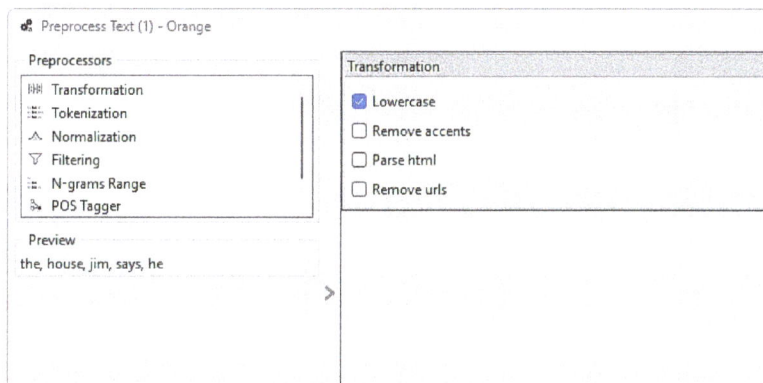

Next attach a Corpus viewer widget to the Preprocess Text widget and open it to view.

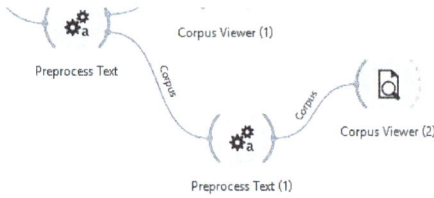

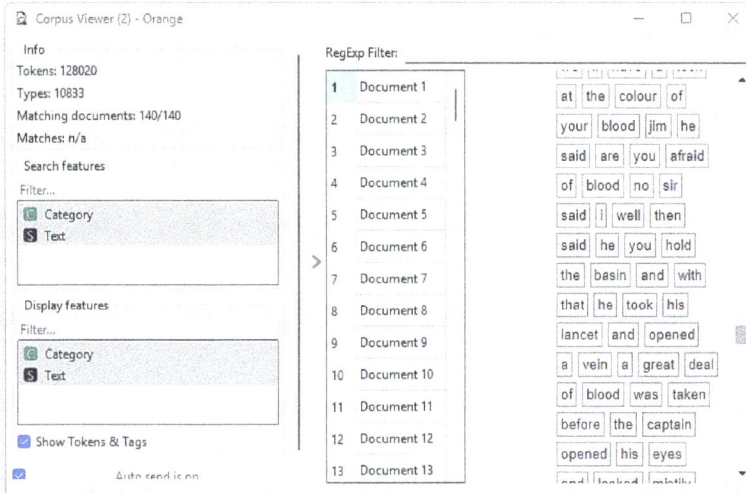

All the text is lowercase (scroll around and compare to what you see in the first Preprocess text corpus viewer).

The last thing we will do is remove stopwords. Stopwords are common words like "the," "and," or "is" that appear often. Because they are common words that appear everywhere that contribute nothing to analytics of the meaning of text. Removing them lets the important words stand out in your analysis.

Add a third Preprocess Text widget to the first. Open it and add Filtering stop words to the right-side selections to preprocess. IMPORTANT Orange needs an actual list of stop words to use. It should have a programmed in default list but may not (double check that it is removing stopwords by using a corpus view befor and after this step). An English language stop words list is easy to obtain online make one and put it in a text file or use the stopwords.txt file. Upload this file in the stopwords file option in the filter (without this file the preprocess text will run but no stopwords will be filtered).

```
        ≡    ◄   stopwords.t   ✕        ▶    +

      File    Edit    View

      a
      about
      above
      after
      again
      against
      all
      am
      an
      and
      any
      are
      aren't
      as
      at
      be
      because
      been
      before
      being
      below
      between
      both
      but
      by
      can't
```

Next attach a Corpus viewer widget to this Preprocess Text widget and open it to view.

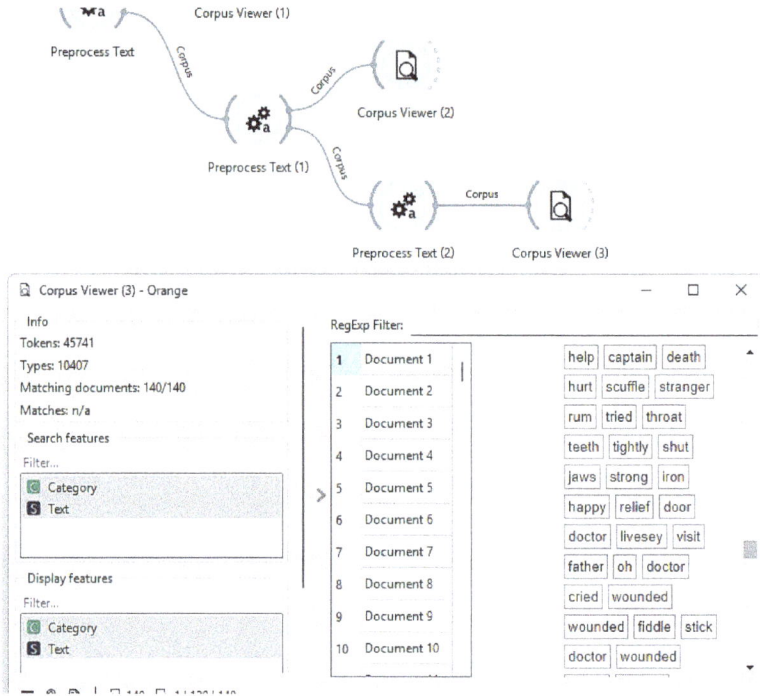

Carefully examine the first document (scroll down to look at the tokens) make sure the check is on the bottom left to show them. The text tokens are now all lower case and all sensible words. This is the preprocessed cleaned text that further analytics can be done on.

Step 3: Visualize Frequencies

In Orange, the Word Cloud widget is a tool that lets you visualize the most frequent words in your text data (at any stage of preprocessing). Add a Word Cloud widget to the third and final Preprocess Text widget and open it.

The cloud shows words in different sizes based on how often they appear across your documents. Words that occur more frequently appear larger and bolder, while less frequent words are smaller. This allows you to instantly see what themes or ideas are most common in your data.

The main purpose of the Word Cloud is exploration. It gives you a quick, visual overview of your text without needing to read through all the documents yourself. It also helps you check that your preprocessing steps worked — if you still see common stopwords like "the" or "and" showing up, it may mean you forgot to remove them. While the Word Cloud doesn't perform deep analysis, it's a very useful way to begin understanding your text and spotting patterns at a glance.

3.2   Wrap-Up

In this lab, you worked with unstructured text data and got a chance to explore how to prepare it for analysis. You installed the Text Mining add-on, loaded a sample corpus, and walked through three major preprocessing steps: tokenizing, lowercasing, and removing stopwords. Each of these steps helped clean up the text so that only the most meaningful words remained.

After preprocessing, you used the Word Cloud widget to visualize the most frequent terms in the dataset. This gave you a quick way to see what kinds of ideas were most common in the sample text. These basic steps are a starting point for more advanced work in text mining.

3.3 Exercises

Unstructured Data

In this exercise, you'll practice working with unstructured data. Load and view each dataset using the Corpus widget, then walk through basic preprocessing steps including tokenization, converting to lowercase, and removing stopwords. Use the Corpus Viewer to observe how the text changes after each step. Try a wordcloud on the final product.

Dataset 1: Social Media Posts

File name: social_posts.csv

1. Load the social_posts.tab file into the Corpus widget. How many documents are in this dataset?

2. What happens in the Corpus Viewer when you check the "Show Tokens & Tags" option?

3. After running tokenization only (using Regexp), paste a screenshot or list showing how tokens appear for the first document.

4. Apply lowercase transformation and view the result in Corpus Viewer. How does the text look now compared to before?

5. Add stopword removal using a basic English list. Share an example of a sentence after stopwords were removed.

Dataset 2: Product Reviews

File name: product_reviews.csv

6. Load this dataset using the Corpus widget and view it in Corpus Viewer. How would you describe the general tone of these reviews?

7. After preprocessing (tokenize + lowercase + stopword removal), use Word Cloud. What are the three most frequent content words you see?

8. Explain why "not" might still be important to keep in some sentiment analysis tasks, even though it is technically a stopword.

9. Show a word cloud after final preprocessing.

10. If you were to build a sentiment classifier (to determine positive or neg-

ative context of the text) from this data later, why would preprocessing steps like these be essential?

Lab 4

Basic Descriptive Statistics

Descriptive statistics (also called summary statistics) are the simple numerical summaries that describe and highlight the main features of a dataset. These include measures of center such as the average (mean), the middle value (median), and the most common value (mode). Descriptive statistics also measure the spread of the data (standard deviation or range), and frequency counts for categories.

In data analytics looking at descriptive statistics early in the analytical process helps spot patterns, outliers, or possible data issues. Such issues can be intervened on before further analysis is carried out.

This lab introduces the basics of exploring a dataset using descriptive statistics in Orange.

4.1 Lesson Steps

Step 1: Load and View the Data

Open Orange, start a new workflow, and drag a Datasets widget onto the canvas. Double-click the Datasets widget to open it, then click Browse and select the dataset named heart-disease.tab (this is built into Orange).

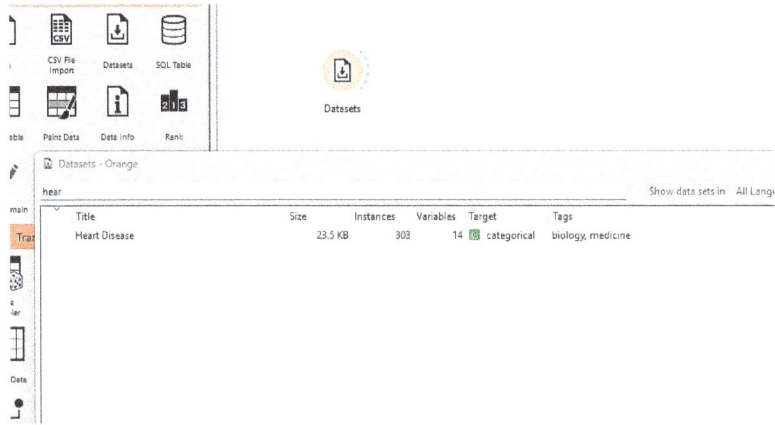

Step 2: Browse the Data

After loading the data, drag a Data Table widget onto the canvas and connect it to the File widget. Finally, double-click the Data Table to view the dataset

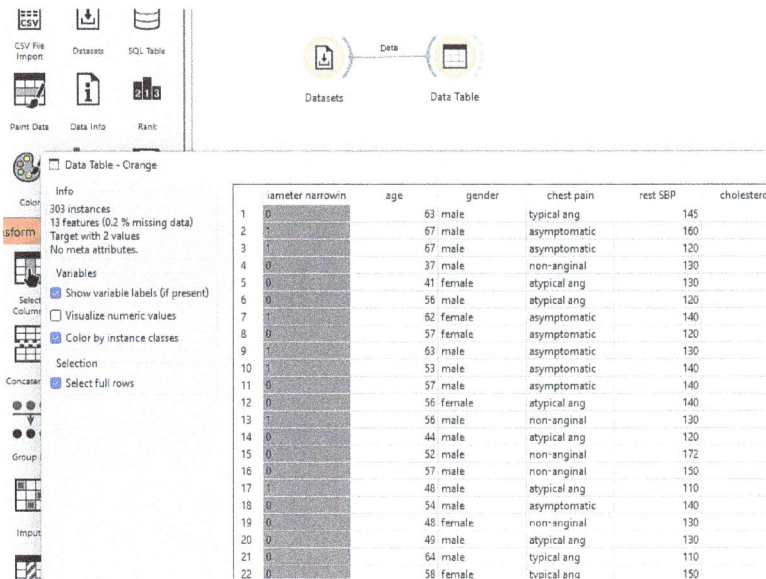

Look over the data and get familiar with the variables and data types by look-ing around the Data Table. Click on the tops of columns to sort the variables low to high or vice versa.

Step 3: Look at Descriptive Statistics

Add a Feature Statistics widget to the workflow and check that the connector says 'Data' not selected data. In data science, a feature is an individual mea-surable property or characteristic of the data being analyzed. Features are the columns in a dataset that represent different types of information about each observation (or row). For example, in a dataset about patients, features might include age, blood pressure, cholesterol level, and gender.

Correct setup is shown here.

Open the Feature Statistics widget. Orange is not super customizable nor is it a statistical program per se (like R and SPSS) because it is really geared to easily doing specific data analytics tasks such as NLP and data mining with-out having to write code. The Feature Statistics display is set to a default that you cannot modify for custom views. However, it is very useful for a quick look at basic statistics in the data and is designed to screen the variables for any issues.

Name	Distribution	Mean	Mode	Median	Dispersion	Min.	Max.	Missing
age		54.44	58	56	0.17	29	77	0 (0 %)
rest SBP		131.69	120	130	0.13	94	200	0 (0 %)
cholesterol		246.69	197	241	0.21	126	564	0 (0 %)
max HR		149.61	162	153	0.15	71	202	0 (0 %)
ST by exercise		1.040	0.0	0.8	1.115	0.0	6.2	0 (0 %)

For numeric variables, Feature statistics give basic descriptive stats. It gives measures of center – mean, median and mode. Then it gives 'Dispersion'. In Orange, dispersion is related to but not the same as standard deviation. Dispersion usually refers to the coefficient of variation (CV), which is the standard deviation divided by the mean. This gives a unit less measure of how spread out the data is relative to its average value, making it easier to compare variability across features with different scales or units. Standard deviation, in contrast, measures spread in the original units of the data, showing how much individual values typically differ from the mean.

For example, if age has a mean of 50 and a standard deviation of 10, the dispersion (CV) is 0.2; if cholesterol has a mean of 200 and a standard deviation of 20, its dispersion is 0.1. Although the standard deviations differ, the dispersion values are on a comparable scale because they represent relative variability. So, when Orange shows "dispersion," it usually means the coefficient of variation rather than the raw standard deviation.

Orange also displays the minimum and maximum values and percentage of the data is missing.

Let's look at categorical feature statistics (scroll down the output view).

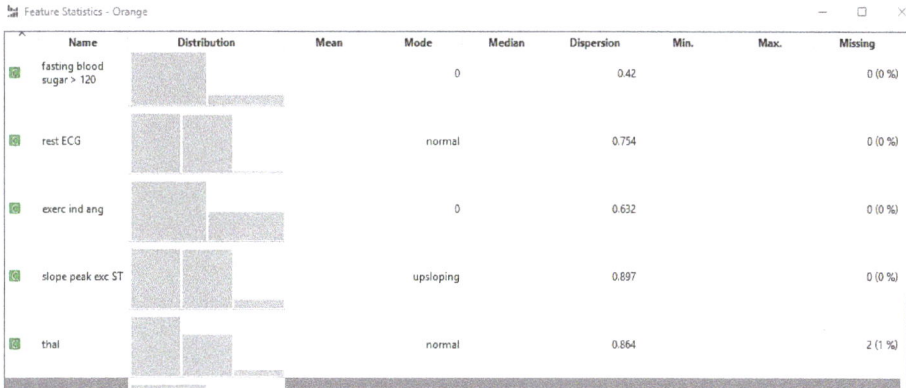

Name	Distribution	Mean	Mode	Median	Dispersion	Min.	Max.	Missing
fasting blood sugar > 120			0		0.42			0 (0 %)
rest ECG			normal		0.754			0 (0 %)
exerc ind ang			0		0.632			0 (0 %)
slope peak exc ST			upsloping		0.897			0 (0 %)
thal			normal		0.864			2 (1 %)

For categorical variables, Orange shows the mode (highest frequency) and percent missing and dispersion. Orange measures dispersion differently for categorical data because standard deviation and similar numeric measures don't apply. Instead, Orange looks at how spread out or varied the categories are. This is usually done by calculating a measure called entropy, which shows how evenly the categories are distributed. If the categories are all about the same size in terms of frequency, entropy is high, meaning more diverse. If one category dominates, entropy is low, meaning less diversity. For categorical features, dispersion tells you how balanced the categories are rather than how much numbers vary.

Step 4: Exploratory Graphs

Under the Visual menu Orange has several graphic widgets. Many of these are highly specialized for specific tasks (such as the silhouette plot, a visual tool used to evaluate how well clusters are formed in a clustering analysis). However, orange does have the usual and common basic exploration graphs useful in descriptive statistics.

Boxplots are the commonly used graph to display distributions that are useful for exploring basic descriptive data. Add a boxplot widget to the Data Table in the workflow. Make sure the connector says "Data" (if not click on the connector – not the widgets themselves – to adjust it).

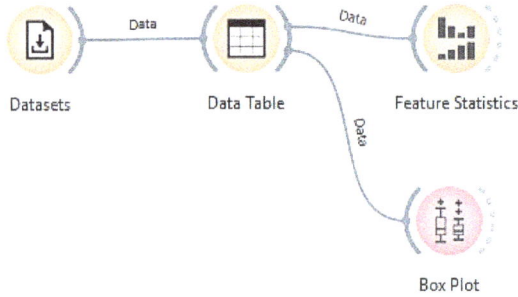

Open the boxplot widget and look at a boxplot of 'ST by exercise', a quantitative variable (likely refers to ST depression induced by exercise relative to rest, a clinical variable often used in heart disease metrics).

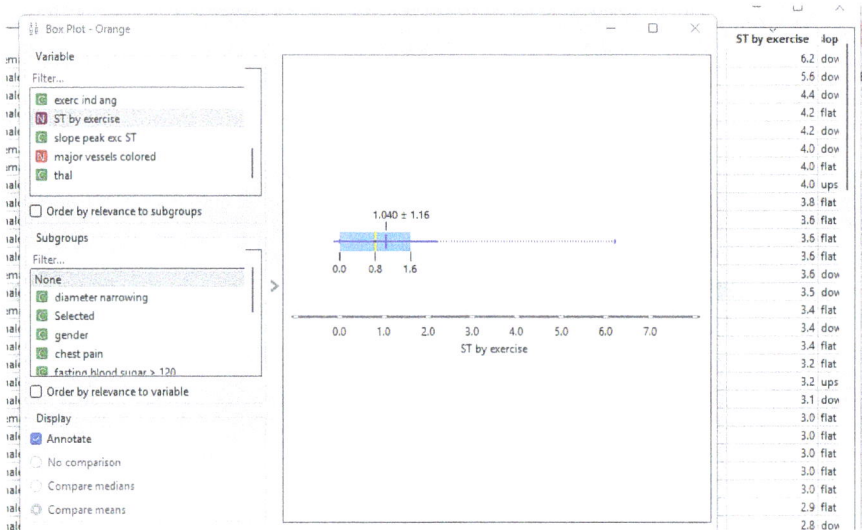

The box plot displays the distribution of the variable "ST by exercise" using descriptive statistics. The mean value is approximately 1.04 with a standard deviation of 1.16. Most values fall between 0.0 and 2.0, as shown by the interquartile range (IQR). The median lies near the lower end of the range, suggesting a right-skewed distribution. Several outliers are present beyond the upper whisker.

4.2 Wrap-Up

In this lab, you practiced working with descriptive statistics using Orange's tools. Descriptive statistics give you a first glance at how your data behaves. They don't answer deep questions, but they are very important to look at as if something looks off at this stage—like extreme outliers or missing values—it's easier to fix now than later.

4.3 Exercises

Descriptive Statistics

Load each dataset and explore it with the Data Table. Use the Feature Statistics widget to find key values like mean, median, and dispersion. Visual tools like Box Plot can help you see patterns. Answer the questions by interpreting what the numbers and graphs show. When asked, include screenshots or explanations.

Dataset 1: employee-retention.tab

This dataset contains information about employees in a tech company, including job role, department, salary, years at the company, and whether the employee left the job (yes/no).

1. What is the mean and dispersion of the variable "Years at Company"?

2. Which categorical variable is the most balanced across categories?

3. What does the distribution of "Satisfaction Score" look like (e.g., symmetric, skewed)?

4. Are there any variables with a high percentage of missing values? Which ones?

5. Does "Salary Level" appear to be associated with variation in "Years at Company"?

Dataset 2: student-performance.tab

This dataset includes performance and demographic information for high school students, such as test scores, study time, absences, and parental education.

6. What is the median value of the variable "Study Time"?

7. Is the variability of "Final Exam Score" high or low based on dispersion?

8. What pattern do you observe in "Absences" by "Parental Education"?

9. Which numeric variable has the largest range (max – min)?

10. What does the mode of the "School Support" variable suggest about the most common category?

Lab 5

Bayes Theorem

Bayes' Theorem is a simple but powerful way to update what we believe based on new evidence using simple probability. Imagine you want to figure out how likely something is to be true, given that you've seen some clues or data. Bayes' Theorem helps you do just that—it combines what you already know (called a "prior belief") with the new information you've observed. It's especially useful in situations where we deal with uncertainty, like diagnosing a disease, filtering spam emails, or making predictions.

Let's explore understanding Bayes Theorem using Orange.

5.1   Lesson Steps

Step 1: Load Dataset

Open Orange and start a new workflow. Add a Datasets widget. Double-click the Datasets widget and select the built-in dataset titanic.

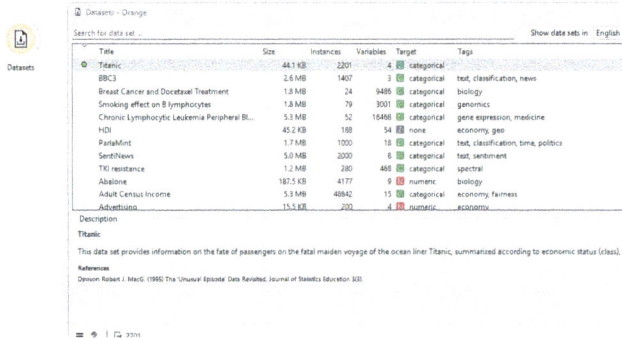

Step 2: Look at the Data

Connect a data table widget to the workflow and open it to look at the data.

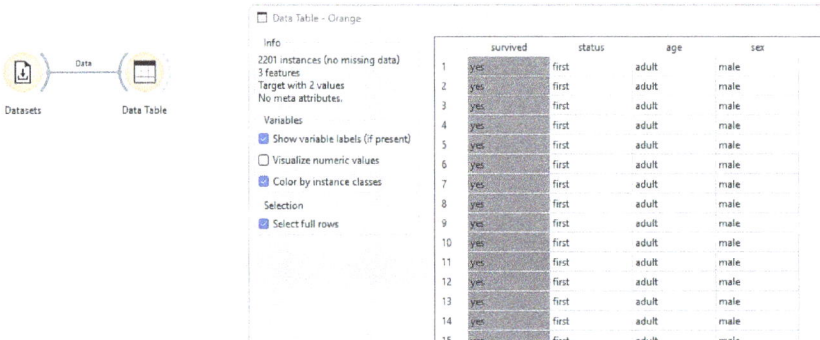

Step 3: Set Target Variable

The target variable is our outcome variable (the 'y' variable in algebra). We want to make sure it's set to survived. Add a Select Columns widget to the workflow. Open it and set the target and feature variable (we will use the variable sex as we will look at survival by gender).

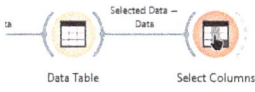

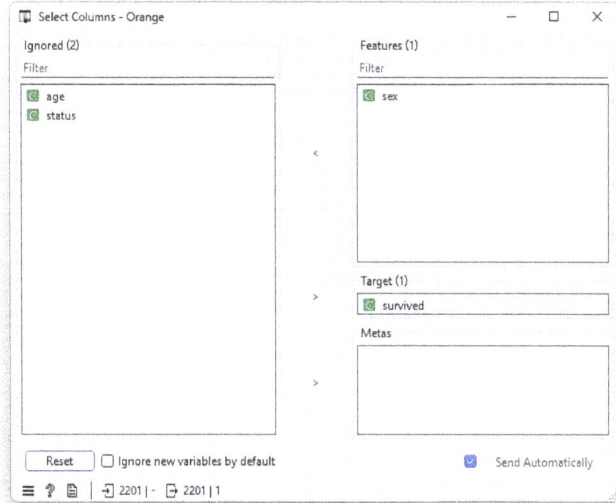

Step 4: Create Subpopulation

Add a Select Rows widget and have it selected for females.

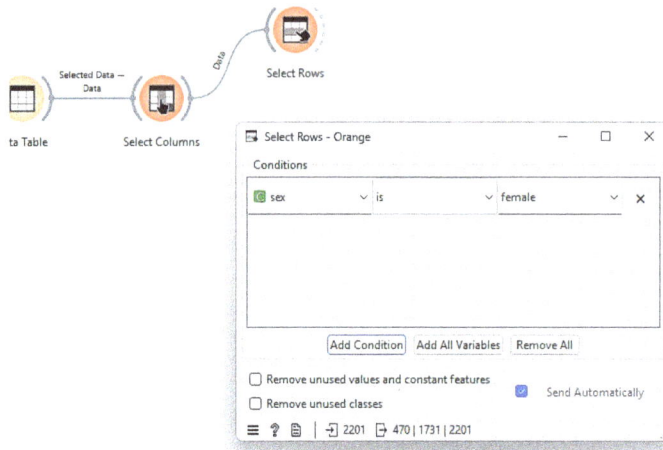

Step 5: Look at Subpopulation Distribution

Add a Distribution widget to the select rows widget and open it with options depicted here. This is giving the basic analytics on the females in terms of the distribution of survivors and non survivors.

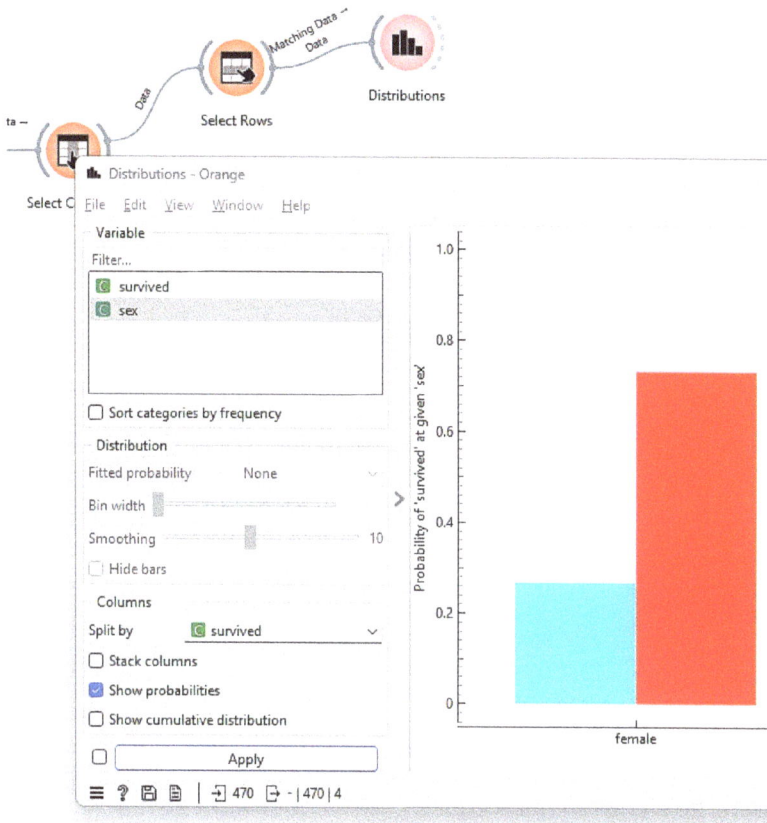

Notice the percentage of females who survive can be estimated from the graph between 70 and 75% (exact percentage can be obtained by carefully hovering over it and result is 73%). This is the concept of conditional probability P(survive | female) = 0.73.

Step 6: Set up the Bayes Classifier

To begin, add these two widgets to the canvas, Naive Bayes, and Test & Score. Next, connect the Select columns (with full not subset by rows data) widget to the Test & Score widget. This sends the Titanic dataset to be used for training and testing.

Then, connect the Naive Bayes widget to the Test & Score widget. This provides the learning algorithm that will be used to make predictions. Do not connect the Select columns widget directly to the Naive Bayes widget — doing so will not run the model or produce any results.

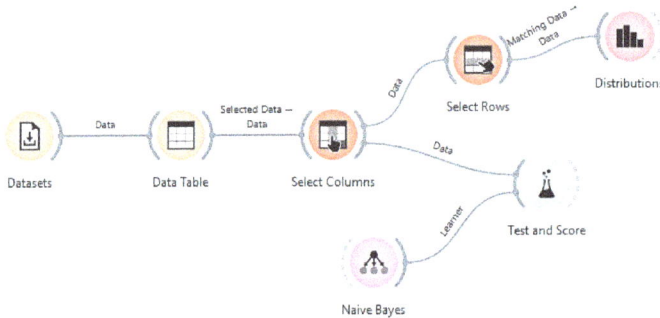

This setup tells Orange to use the Naive Bayes algorithm.

Step 7: Look at Results

(If results are not as shown go back to Step 3 and make sure your features and target are set correctly.)

Behind the scenes, the Naive Bayes model uses Bayes' Theorem to calculate the probability that a passenger survived based on sex (gender). This allows us to evaluate how well Bayes' Theorem works for this real-world problem. Double click on the Test and Score widget and make sure it is set to Cross Validation with n=10 (the specifics of model evaluation and the details are beyond the scope of this course and covered in a full data mining course).

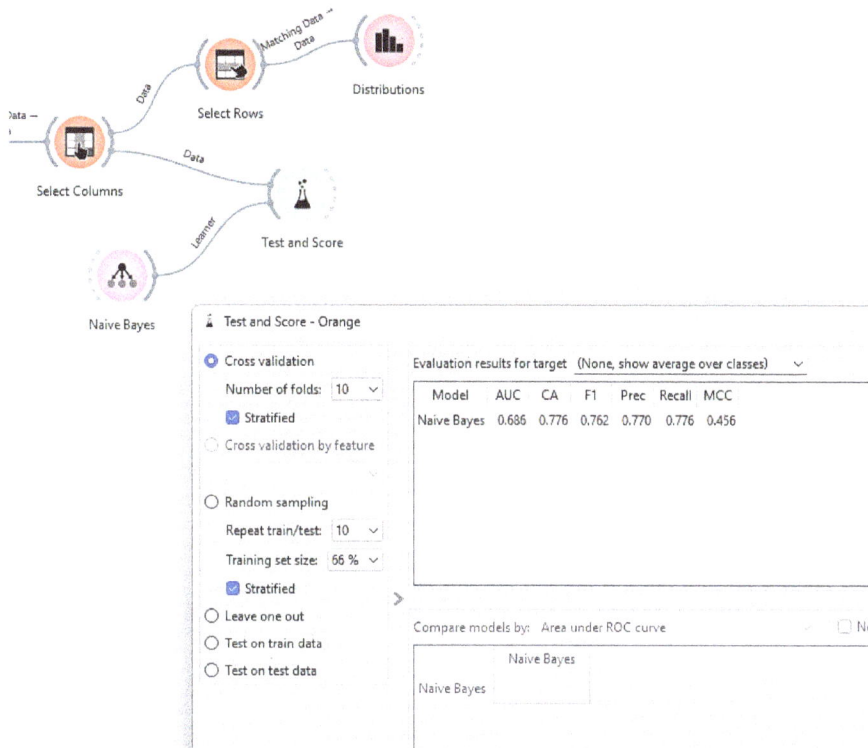

One of the numbers is 'CA' which stands for classification accuracy. This number is 0.776. This means that overall if using gender as a classifier the Bayes got it correct 77.6% of the time if the person survived.

Step 8: Results Continued

Connect a confusion matrix to the Test and score widget and open it.

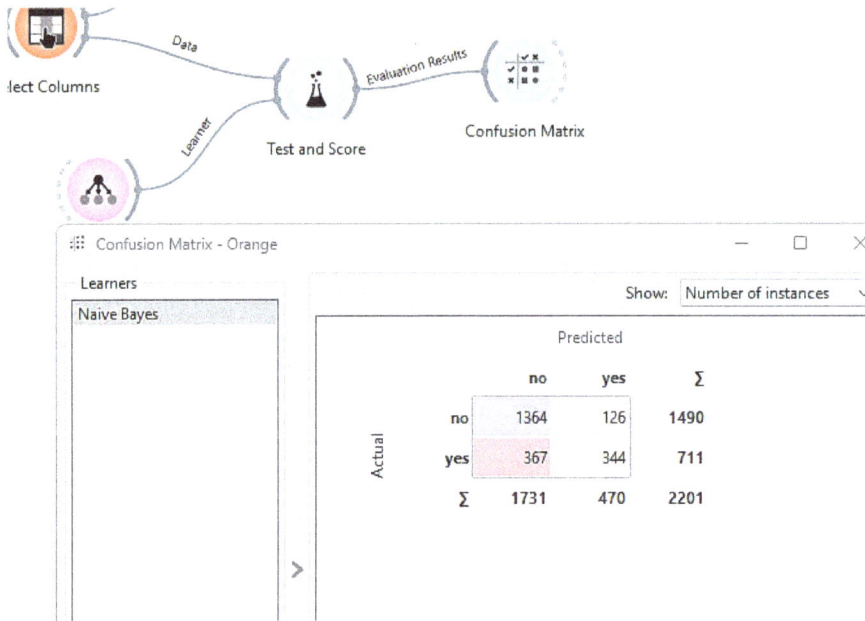

In this example, we used Bayes' Theorem to estimate the probability of survival on the Titanic based on one feature: a passenger's gender (M or F). By calculating the probability of surviving given that a passenger is female or male, the model learned that women had a much higher chance of survival—about 73%—compared to men. This probability was found using Bayes' Theorem, which combines the overall survival rate with the likelihood of being female among survivors and the overall proportion of females on board.

$$P(\text{Survived} \mid \text{Female}) = \frac{P(\text{Female} \mid \text{Survived}) \cdot P(\text{Survived})}{P(\text{Female})}$$

From the data:

- $P(\text{Female} \mid \text{Survived}) = \frac{344}{711} \approx 0.484$

- $P(\text{Survived}) = \frac{711}{2201} \approx 0.323$

- $P(\text{Female}) = \frac{470}{2201} \approx 0.214$

Plugging these into the formula:

$$P(\text{Survived} \mid \text{Female}) \approx \frac{0.484 \times 0.323}{0.214} \approx 0.73$$

A similar calculation was performed for males. The model then used these probabilities to make predictions: if a passenger was female, it predicted "Survived"; if male, "Did Not Survive."

The confusion matrix summarizes how well these predictions matched the actual outcomes. Out of 470 passengers predicted to survive (all females), 344 did, and 126 did not. Out of 1,731 passengers predicted not to survive (all males), 1,364 didn't, but 367 did survive. In total, the model made 1,708 correct predictions out of 2,201, resulting in an accuracy of about 77.6%. This shows how Bayes' Theorem was applied to make simple, rule-based predictions based on observed survival patterns in the data.

5.2   Wrap-Up

Bayes' Theorem can help update our understanding of likelihoods based on new information. Using the Titanic dataset, we calculated the probability of survival given a passenger's gender. By looking at the confusion matrix, we saw how well a Bayes classifier model guesses matched the actual outcomes. Although this was a simple example it demonstrated how Bayes' Theorem works in practice. Bayes theorem is a tool for dealing with uncertainty and making decisions based on partial information.

5.3   Exercises

Bayes' Theorem

These exercises will practice Bayes Theorem.

Dataset 1: loan-approval.tab

This fictional dataset includes basic information about people who applied for a loan, such as their income, credit score, employment status, and whether the loan was approved.

1. For people who are employed, what percentage were approved for a loan?

2. How accurate is the model when using only EmploymentStatus to predict loan approval?

3. Look at the confusion matrix. Did the model make more mistakes by approving people who should not be approved, or by rejecting people who should be approved?

4. What percentage of all people in the dataset were approved for a loan?

5. In your own words, how does the model use EmploymentStatus to make predictions about loan approval?

Dataset 2: reviews-keyword.tab

This dataset contains short product reviews along with a column showing whether the word "excellent" appears in the review and another column showing whether the review is positive or negative.

6. Look at the reviews where the word "excellent" appears. What percentage of those reviews are positive?

7. When using only the keyword "excellent" to predict whether a review is positive, how accurate is the model?

8. In the confusion matrix, how many negative reviews were wrongly predicted as positive?

9. Do most reviews contain the word "excellent," or is it only used in a small number of them?

10. Do you think the word "excellent" is a good clue for deciding whether a review is positive? Why or why not?

Lab 6

Distributions

In this lab, you'll explore how data is distributed. Many analytical methods depend on data distributed in particular ways such as the normal distribution so being able to assess whether data is normally distributed or not is important. Also exploring data distribution early in analysis can help pinpoint issues and troubles in the data (such as outlies or bimodal populations which should be analyzed separately).

We will look at both numeric and categorical variables to understand how values are spread out, how often they appear, and what that tells you about patterns in the data. Orange's many distribution tools—like histograms, box plots, and violin plots— will be explored to assess shape and variability of your data.

6.1   Lesson Steps

Step 1: Load the Dataset

The Adult Income dataset (which comes with Orange when you download it - note you may have to do a search to find the folder containing this file on your computer) will be used here. This data contains information about individuals, including numeric features like age, education level (in years), hours worked per week, and financial factors such as capital gains and losses.

Open Orange. Drag a File widget onto the canvas. Click the File widget and load the Adult.CSV file.

Step 2: Overview with Data Table

Drag a Data Table widget and connect it to File widget.

	age	workclass	fnlwgt	education	education.num	marital.status	oc
1	90	?	77053	HS-grad	9	Widowed	?
2	82	Private	132870	HS-grad	9	Widowed	Exec-
3	66	?	186061	Some-college	10	Widowed	?
4	54	Private	140359	7th-8th	4	Divorced	Mach
5	41	Private	264663	Some-college	10	Separated	Prof-:
6	34	Private	216864	HS-grad	9	Divorced	Other
7	38	Private	150601	10th	6	Separated	Adm-
8	74	State-gov	88638	Doctorate	16	Never-married	Prof-:
9	68	Federal-gov	422013	HS-grad	9	Divorced	Prof-:
10	41	Private	70037	Some-college	10	Never-married	Craft-
11	45	Private	172274	Doctorate	16	Divorced	Prof-:
12	38	Self-emp-not-inc	164526	Prof-school	15	Never-married	Prof-:
13	52	Private	129177	Bachelors	13	Widowed	Other
14	32	Private	136204	Masters	14	Separated	Exec-
15	51	?	172175	Doctorate	16	Never-married	?

Open the Data Table to inspect variables.

Step 3: Add a Distributions widget

From the Visualize menu add a Distributions widget and connect it to the File widget. Make sure the connector says 'Data' if not fix this by clicking on connector and set the flow to 'Data'.

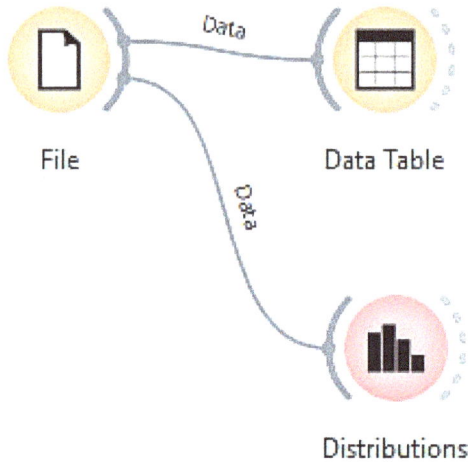

Step 4: Look at Distributions

Inspect the variables step-by-step. Variable types are listed. For categorical variables such as relationship the distributions show how often each category appears in the data. It looks like a bar chart (but technically is a histogram), where each bar represents one category, and the height of the bar shows the number (or percentage) of observations in that category. This graph helps you quickly see which categories are most common, which categories are rare, and whether the data is balanced or skewed toward certain groups which is clear from how symmetric the plot is.

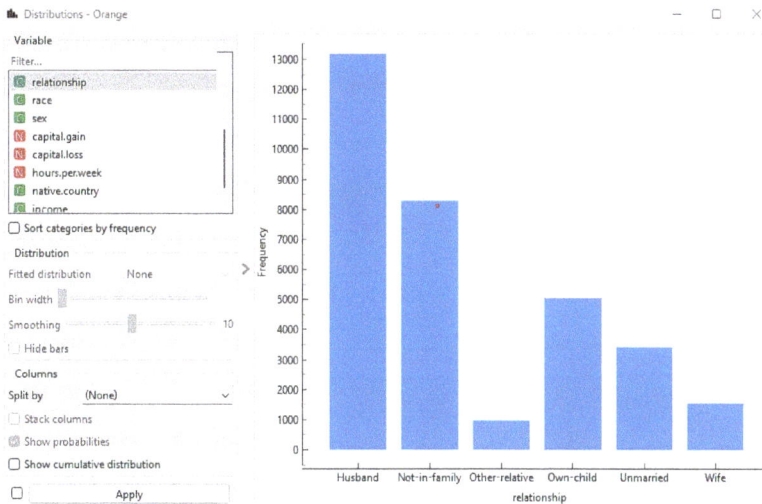

For example, if you have a categorical variable for "relationship" the distribution graph will show how many people fall into each category – single, married, etc.

For numeric variables Orange creates bins grouping the quantitative data. This is because quantitative data usually can take on an infinite spectrum of values (unless it's very simple discrete count data with a limited range). Displaying such data usually requires grouping or 'binning'. Bins can be adjusted using the slide on the left side. For example, if we pull up age and the bin width is set to 50 we get this result.

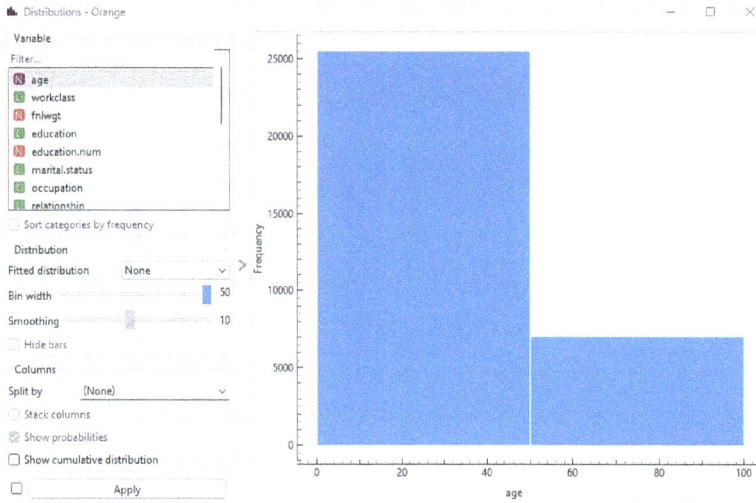

Grouping the data in bins of 50 for age is not very informative. Adjust the bin to 5 and get a more informative view of the age distribution.

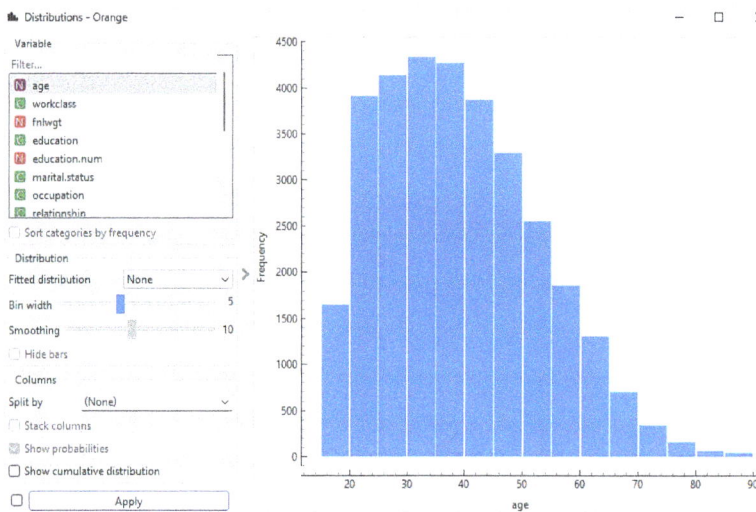

Age is roughly (although not perfectly) symmetric for this distribution and may meet the requirement of being normally distributed for statistical purposes.

The distribution for capital gains, however, is strongly right skewed. A right-skewed distribution is one where most of the data values are clustered on the left side, with a long tail stretching to the right, meaning a few values are much higher than the rest. This is a common distribution for financial data to be right skewed (as few people are in high financial metrics and most in low).

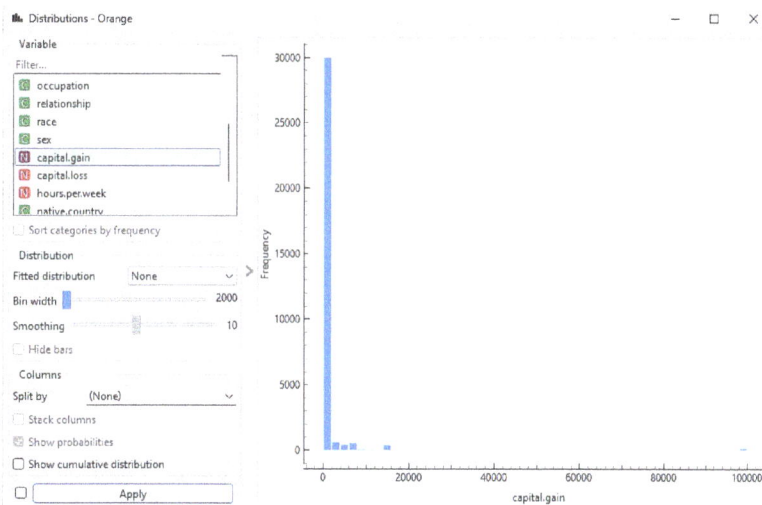

Step 5: Look at Box Plots

A histogram and a box plot both show information about a variable's distribution, but they serve different purposes. A histogram is best for showing the overall shape of the data. It groups values into bins and displays how frequently each occurs, making it easy to see if the data is bell-shaped (normal), skewed, or has multiple peaks. This makes histograms ideal for checking whether a variable looks approximately normal or a bimodal or skewed distribution.

A box plot summarizes the distribution using the five-number summary: minimum, first quartile (Q1), median, third quartile (Q3), and maximum. Box plots are great for comparing the spread of different groups (such as comparing male vs female). Boxplots also are superior to histograms in spotting outliers, which are shown as dots outside the "whiskers."

Box plots also are only good for numeric data whereas distributions plotted with the Distribution widget can do categorical distributions as well (there is no five number summary of non-numerical data).

Add a box plot widget to the workflow.

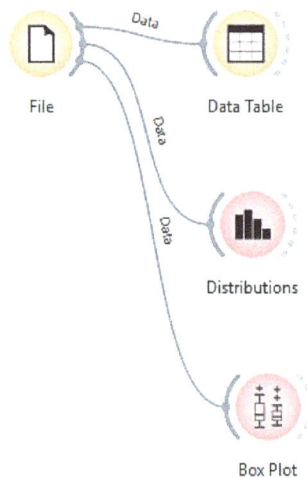

Let's look at a boxplot of hours worked. Open the boxplot and select this variable. Also make sure annotate is checked off under display (which puts five number summary metrics on the plot).

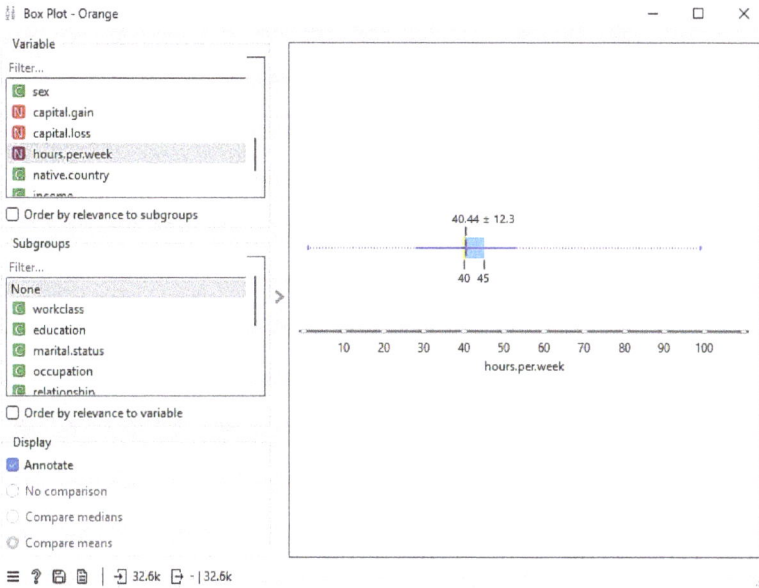

Hours worked is quite symmetrical. The IQR (25th to 75th percentiles or middle of the data) is quite tight in range and shows most people work a standard 40ish hour workweek.

Let's look at a box plot of capital gains.

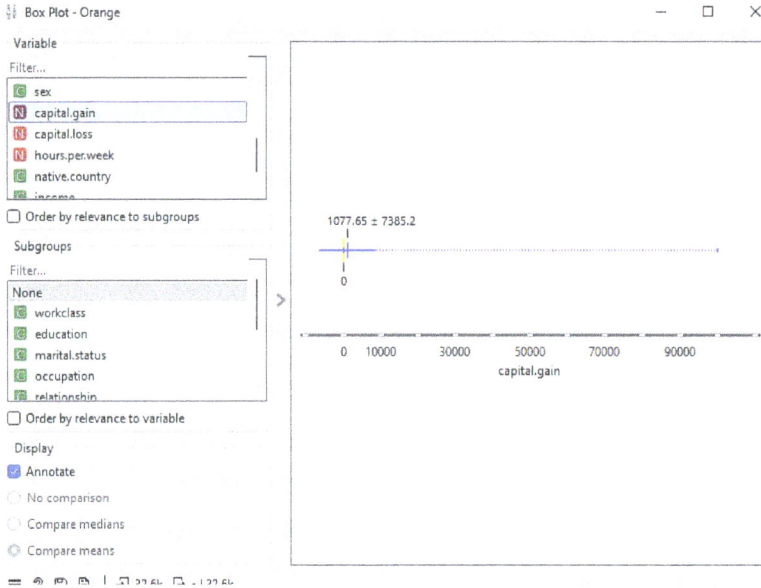

The right skew of the distribution for capital gains (as seen in the prior bar style distribution chart) is evident.

Step 6: Violin Plots

Orange has another plot to view distributions called a violin plot. A violin plot offers more detail than a box plot, especially when you want to understand the shape of the distribution—not just the summary statistics. While a box plot shows the median, quartiles, and potential outliers, it doesn't reveal how the data is distributed within those quartiles.

A violin plot includes all that plus a smoothed density curve on each side, which shows where the data is more concentrated or spread out. For example, if a variable has two common values (a bimodal distribution), a box plot will miss that—but a violin plot will show two bulges where the data clusters. Compared to violin plots, box plots are simpler and easier to read briefly, especially when comparing many groups. Also, boxplots are far more common so people will be familiar with them whereas violin plots are somewhat obscure.

Add a violin plot to the workflow.

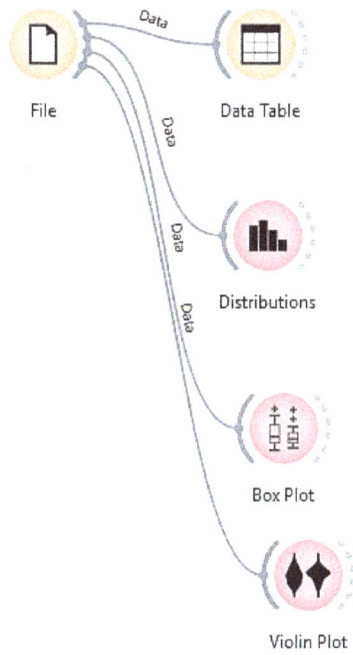

Let's do a violin plot of age.

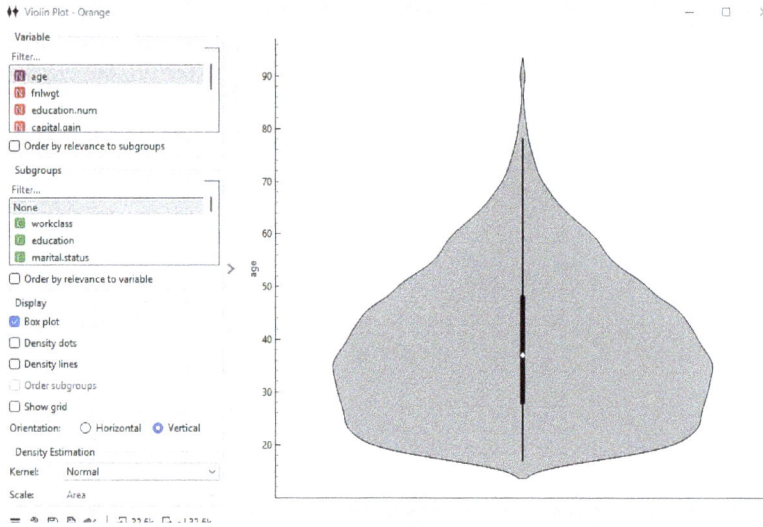

And a violin plot of capital gains.

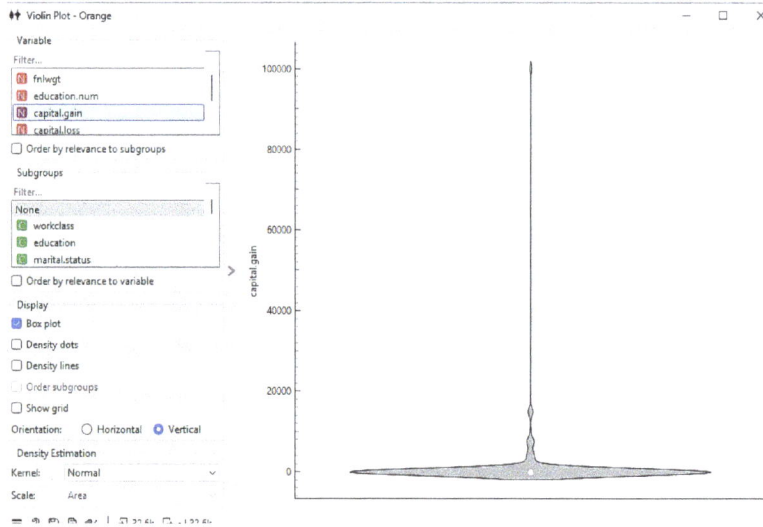

The violin plot provides a clear summary of the data distribution, combining a box plot's summary statistics with a density curve.

6.2 Wrap-Up

By the end of this lab, you have experience using Orange to look at patterns in distributions. You learned how histograms show the shape of numeric data, how box plots summarize values and highlight outlines, and how violin plots combine both ideas for a more detailed view. These tools help you decide whether data is symmetric, skewed, or has unusual gaps or peaks. Looking at distributions of data is always important in understanding the data you are analyzing.

6.3 Exercises

Understanding Distributions

In this exercise, you'll explore how variables are distributed using Orange. Start by opening each dataset in Orange. Use the Data Table to preview the data, then add Distribution, Box Plot, and Violin Plot widgets to help answer each question.

Dataset 1: health-lifestyle.tab

This dataset includes self-reported health and lifestyle data for individuals, such as sleep hours, exercise frequency, smoking status, and weight.

1. What is the most common ExerciseLevel based on the distribution?

2. Is the distribution of SleepHours symmetric or skewed?

3. Are there any outliers in Weight according to the box plot?

4. What does the violin plot of SleepHours show about the shape of its distribution?

5. Is SmokingStatus balanced across categories or dominated by one group?

Dataset 2: college-stats.tab

This dataset contains institutional statistics such as average GPA, class size, number of majors, and whether the college is private or public.

6. Which InstitutionType is more common: Public or Private?

7. What is the shape of the distribution of ClassSize?

8. Is the AvgGPA data tightly clustered or widely spread out based on the box plot?

9. Does the violin plot of ClassSize show one mode or multiple modes?

10. Which visualization helped you better understand GPA differences—box plot or violin plot—and why?

Lab 7

Correlations and Scatterplots

Correlations and scatterplots help us understand how two quantitative variables relate. A scatterplot provides a visual display of a relationship between two variables, while correlation coefficient gives a numerical summary of the strength and direction of that relationship. In this lab, you will explore both correlations and scatterplots.

7.1 Lesson Steps

Step 1 Load the Dataset

Launch Orange and create a new workflow. Add a file widget to the workflow. Click the widget and load the fish.csv dataset.

Step 2: View the Data

Find and drag a Data Table widget onto the canvas. Connect the File widget to Data Table widget by clicking and dragging from the right edge of File to the left edge of Data Table to hook up a connector. Double-click Data Table to inspect the data.

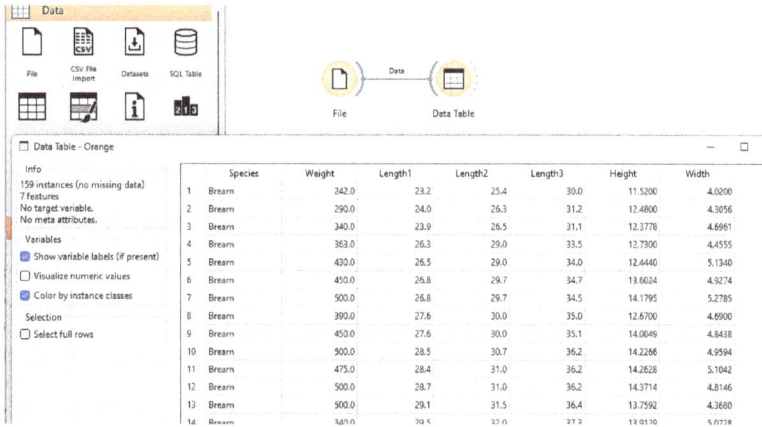

Step 3: Look at Scatterplots

A scatterplot is a simple, yet powerful graph used to explore the relationship between two numerical variables. Each point on the plot represents a single observation, with its position determined by the values of the two variables. By looking at the overall pattern of the points, we can see whether there is a positive, negative, or no clear relationship between the variables. Scatterplots help us spot trends, clusters, and outliers, and they are often the first step in understanding correlation or deciding whether a linear model might be appropriate.

Add a Scatter Plot widget to the workflow and connect it to the Data Table. Make sure the connector says "Data" (if not adjust it).

Next open the Scatter Plot widget. In the Scatter Plot window, set the X-axis to Length3 and the Y-axis to Weight.

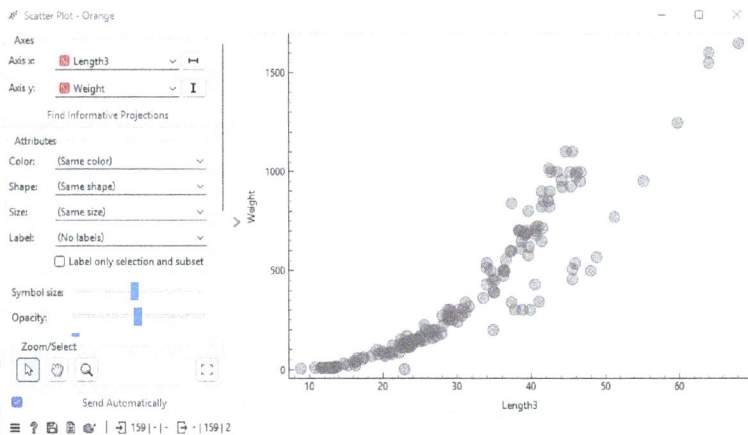

Currently the scatter plot is of the complete (all species) data and exhibits a nonlinear trend. However, to make things a little more interesting select under attributes color 'species'. Now the graph appears to have positive linear trends for each species which is color coded by species.

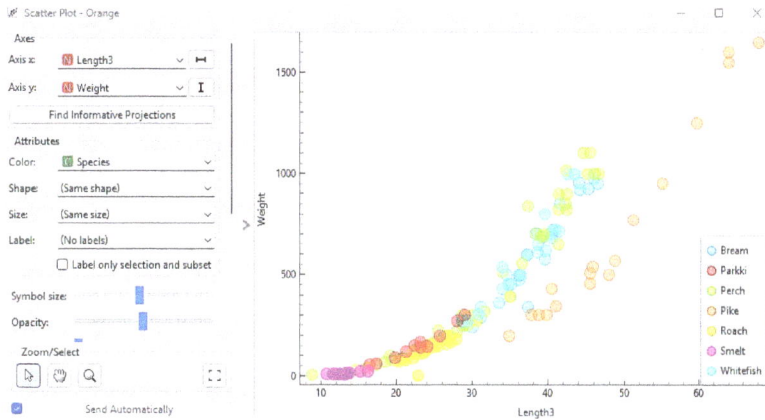

Scatterplots can be very helpful in viewing relations between data. Here we also see that it matters if you look at all the data vs look at the data by individual species. Different fish species are quite different in their size and relation of length and weight.

Step 4: Measure Correlations

A correlation is a metric to describe how two numerical variables move in relation to each other. When we talk about correlation in statistics, we are usually referring to Pearson's correlation coefficient, which measures the strength and direction of a linear relationship between two quantitative variables.

The value of the correlation coefficient ranges from -1 to +1. A value close to +1 means that the two variables increase together in a straight-line pattern. This is considered a strong positive linear correlation. A value close to -1 means that as one variable increases, the other decreases. This is a strong negative linear correlation. A value close to 0 suggests little or no linear relationship between the variables.

It's important to be aware that linear correlation only measures linear relationships, or how well the data points follow a straight line. If the relationship is non-linear then Pearson's correlation might not detect it, even if the variables are strongly related in another way. This is why it's important to look at a scatterplot before interpreting correlation. You need a linear plot of the variables before using Pearson's correlation as a metric to describe the relation.

To compute at the overall correlation in the data, add a Correlation widget to the Data Table and open it.

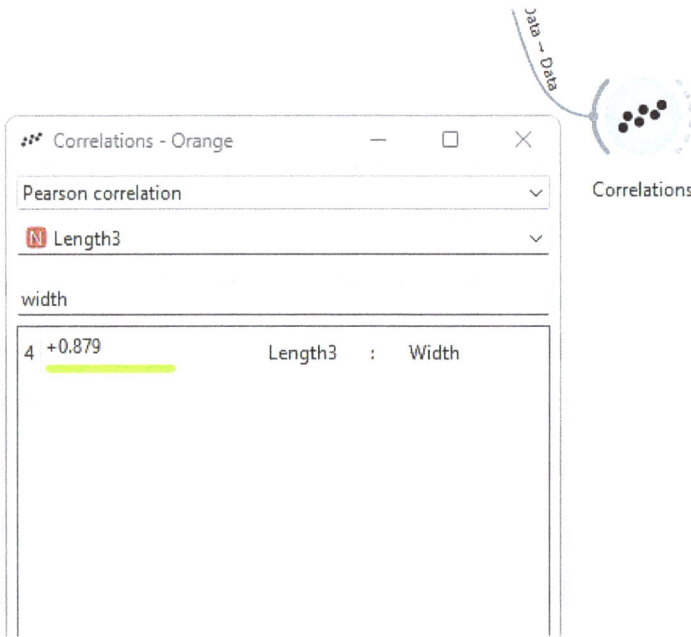

There is a strong positive correlation value of 0.879 however this is for the pooled (all species) data. However, since the relations within each fish species between length and weight appear even more linear than the overall relation it would be important to measure correlation only within each individual species.

Step 5: Looking at Specific Correlations

Let's setup to look at correlations for each individual species. Add a Select Rows widget connected to the data table. Next add a correlations widget and connect it to the Select Rows widget. Add a Scatter Plot widget connected to the Correlation widget and set the connector as depicted (to say matching data).

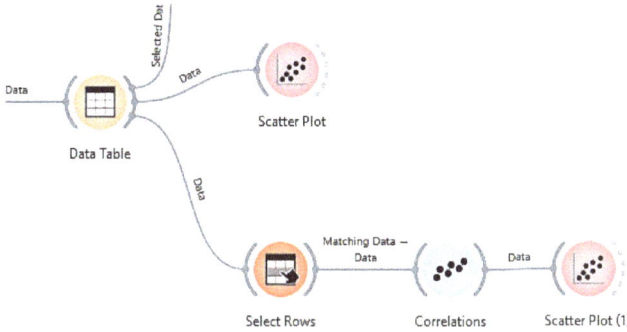

Next open and position the Select Rows, Correlation and Scatterplot widgets so you can see all 3 widgets. They will open to defaults. Note in the correlation widget a filter for width has been added and it has been set to Length 3 by width (this will show only this correlation as there are many) and for the scatterplot the color by species has been applied.

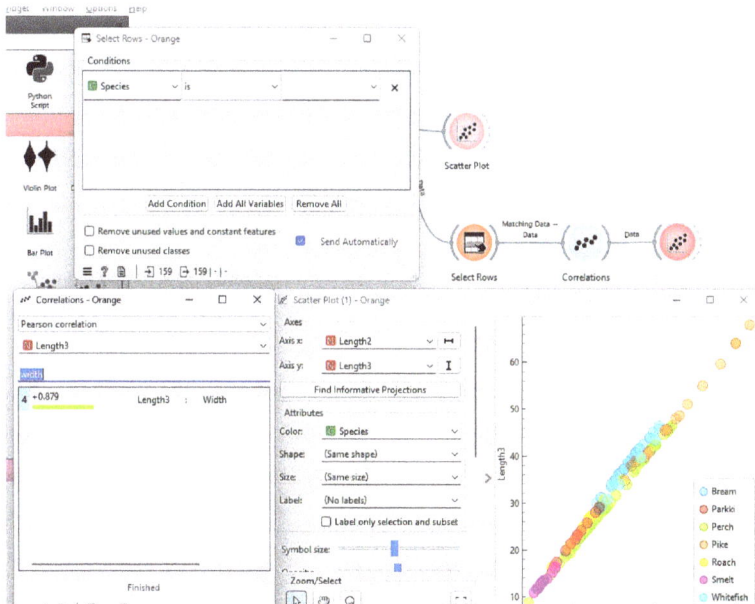

Effectively this has created an active view where the species can be changed in the Select row by the condition species is (and setting the drop-down condition). Orange is great for doing things like this where you can dynamically look at 'what if' and specific data situations. When a species filter for the Select Row is applied the correlation and scatterplot will update and show this species only, as is shown below for the species Pike.

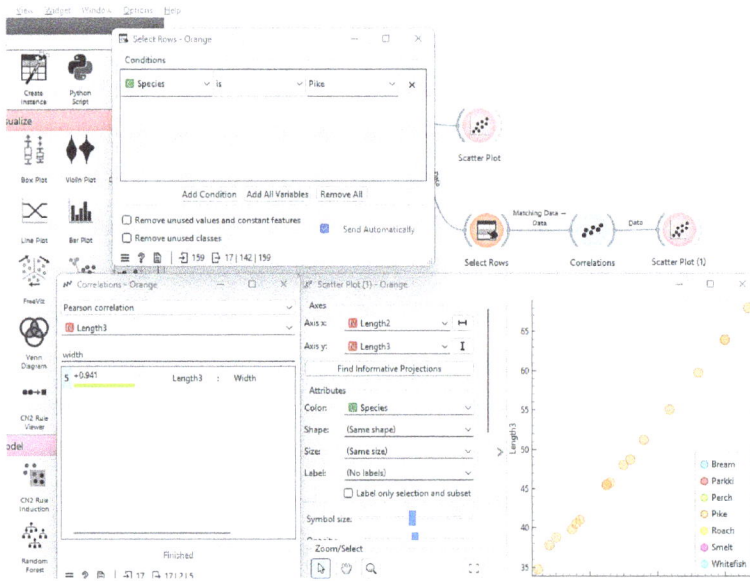

This type of workflow is easy to setup in Orange and allows for efficient and interactive investigation of patterns in data.

7.2   Wrap-Up

You now have a better understanding of how to explore relationships between variables using both scatterplots and correlations. You saw how the overall trend in a dataset can sometimes mask patterns that only become clear when data is separated by group. Using Orange's interactive tools, you built a setup to explore these patterns more closely.

7.3   Exercises

Correlations and Scatterplots

In this exercise, you'll explore how two variables relate to each other using scatterplots and correlation. Start by loading each dataset into a new Orange workflow. Then use the Scatter Plot and Correlation widgets to examine the patterns between two numeric variables. Try adding color or filters to see how subgroups behave differently. Use the Select Rows widget when prompted to look at specific groups.

Dataset 1: plant-growth.tab

This dataset contains measurements of plant growth under different light and water conditions. It includes numeric variables such as height, number of leaves, and days to sprout, along with treatment group.

1. What is the shape of the relationship between DaysToSprout and Height? Is it linear, curved, or flat?

2. What is the correlation between DaysToSprout and Height in the full dataset?

3. After filtering for Treatment = HighLight, what is the new correlation between DaysToSprout and Height?

4. Does the HighLight group follow a stronger or weaker linear pattern than the full dataset?

5. When coloring the scatterplot by Treatment, what differences in trends or clustering do you observe?

Dataset 2: housing-market.tab

This dataset contains simulated data on housing sales, including square footage, price, number of bedrooms, and whether the home is urban or rural.

6. What kind of relationship exists between SquareFootage and Price according to the scatterplot—positive or negative?

7. What is the Pearson correlation for SquareFootage and Price in the full dataset?

8. What is the correlation between SquareFootage and Price for urban

homes only? How does it compare to the full dataset?

9. Based on the scatterplot, are home prices more consistent (less spread out) in Urban or Rural areas?

10. What does this example show about how grouping data can affect correlation strength?

Lab 8

Linear Regression

Linear regression is a foundation technique in statistics and machine learning. It mathematically models the relationship between one or more input (independent) variables and a single output (dependent) variable when there is a strong linear correlation between the variables. Such models can be used to predict future events. This lab helps you build and interpret both simple and multiple linear regression models in Orange.

8.1 Lesson Steps

Step 1: Load Data

Start by opening the Orange application and creating a new workflow. From the left-hand panel, drag and drop the "File" widget onto the canvas. Double-click the widget to open it and use the folder icon to browse and load the students.csv file.

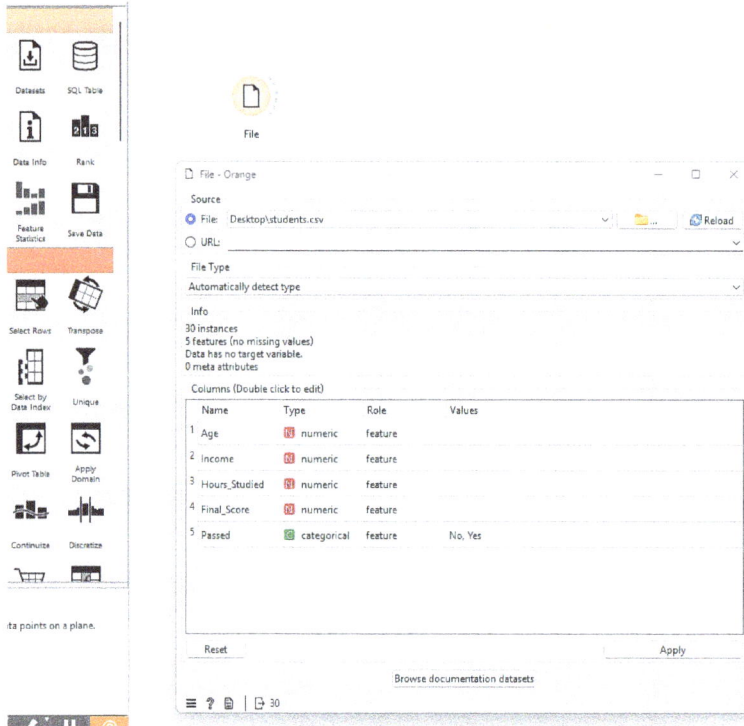

Step 2: Look at the Data

Connect to the File widget a Feature Statistics widget to look over the variables and basic statistics on them. (Another option would be to hook up a Data Table and look at that, but Feature Statistics is more useful here).

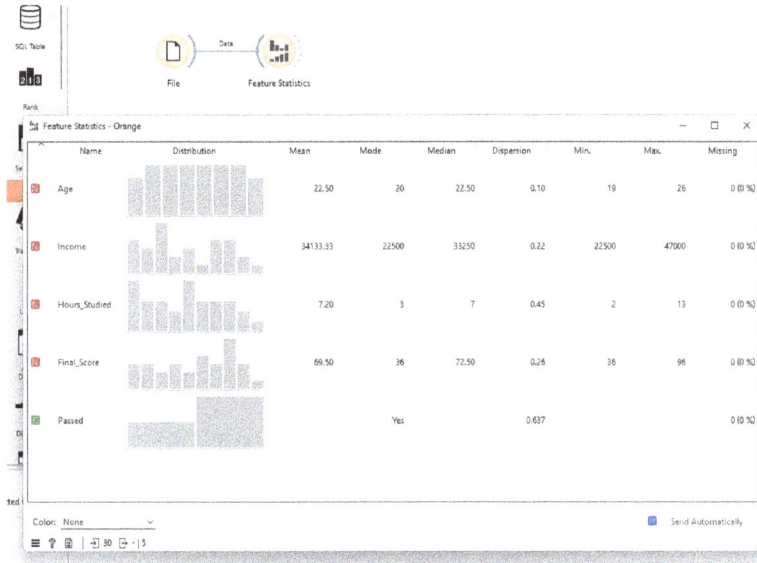

Step 3: Setup Simple Linear Regression

Connect a Select Columns widget to the File widget and open it. Set hours studied as the Feature (input or x variable) and final score as the target (output or y variable).

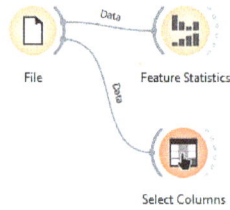

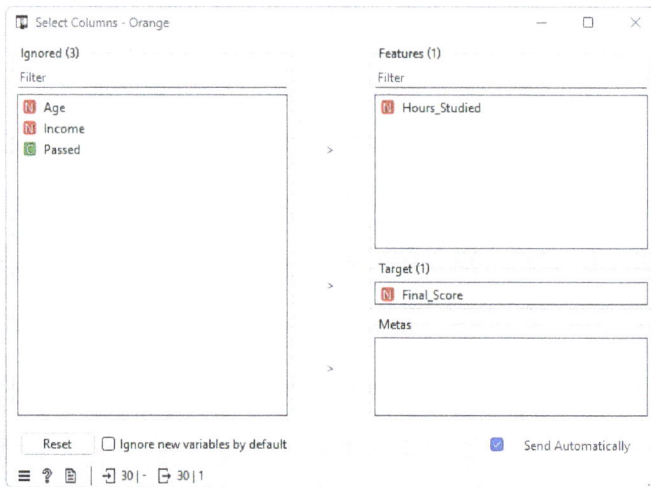

This will setup the workflow to do a simple linear regression. Simple linear regression models the relationship between two variables: one independent (predictor) and one dependent (outcome). It models this relationship with a straight line, typically written as Y=a+bX where a is the intercept and b is the slope.

Note in algebra class m is written as the slope and b the intercept for a linear equation and the line is y=mx+b. Statistics by convention use different variables and the regression model is made by fitting actual data, so it is a slightly different procedure from simply writing an equation of a line.

The slope tells us how much the dependent variable changes for each unit increase in the independent variable. The intercept is the y value when x is zero which may or may not have any interpretative meaning.

Step 4: Look at the relationship of the variables

Before doing linear regression the linearity of the relationship between variables should be verified. Add a Scatterplot widget to the Select Columns widget and open it and set the x and y variables.

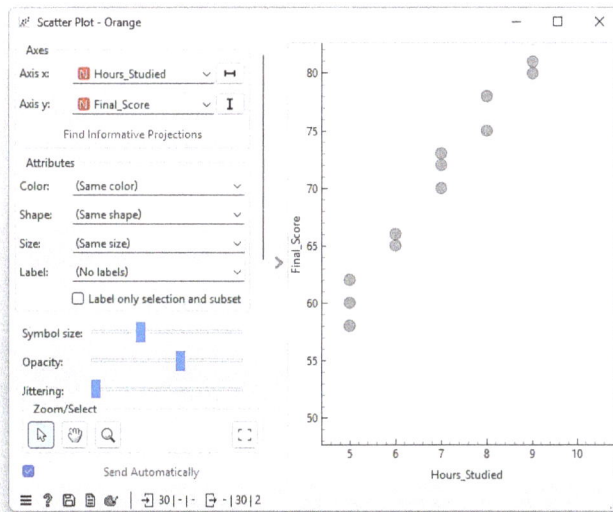

The relation of final score and hours studied looks very linear. Scroll down on the Scatterplot widget to check the option to show the regression line. This puts a regression line (although with no actual equation) on the plot and gives a correlation metric (presumably a Pearson correlation) of 0.99.

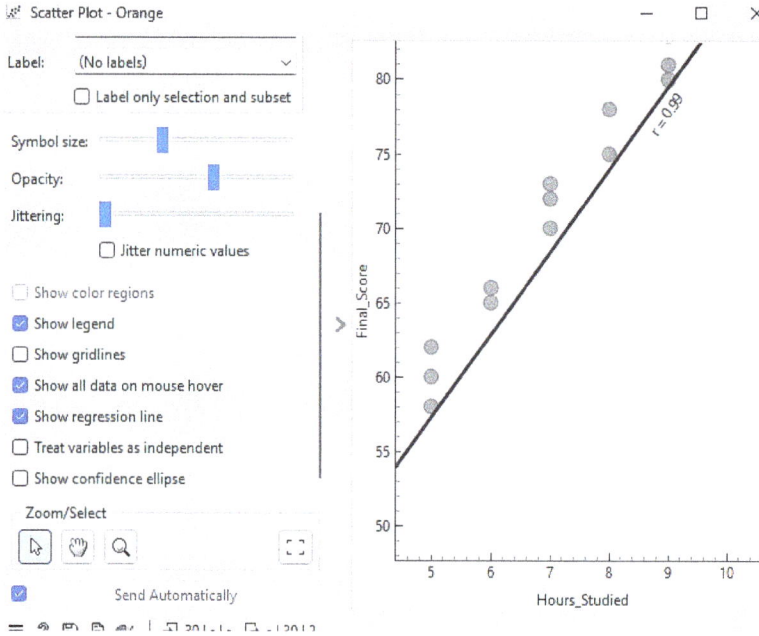

Step 5: Obtain Model Coefficients

First from the Model menu select a Linear Regression widget to add to the workflow and connect this to the Select Columns widget. Open it and it shows the default settings (we will not modify these).

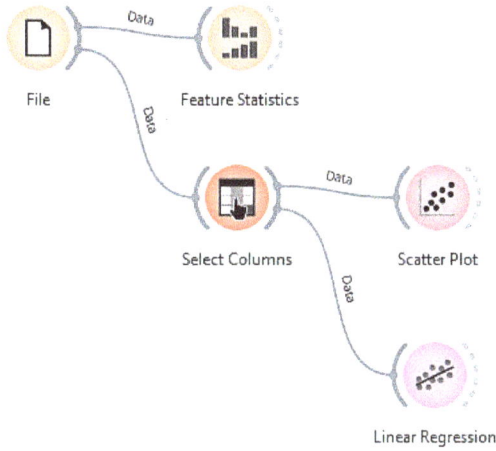

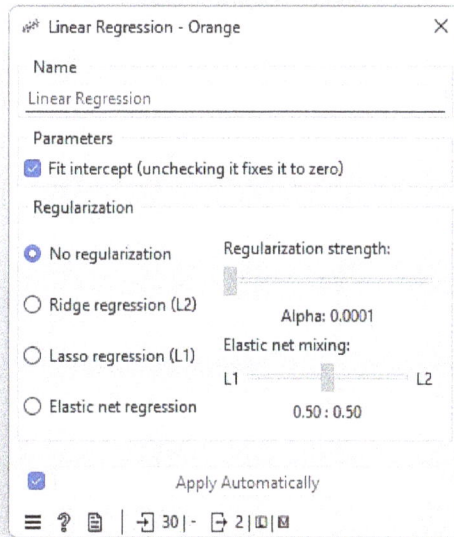

Next connect a Data Table widget to the Linear Regression widget. Make sure the connector to the Data Table widget says 'Coefficients – Data' (if not adjust it on the connector - click specifically on the connector to do so). Open the data table to view the slope and intercept.

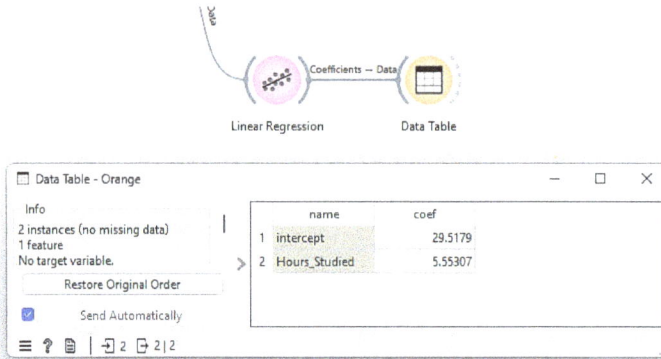

Based on this data a simple linear regression to predict final score given hours studied is that final scores = 29.5 + 5.55 * hours studied. Although we could do further diagnostics given the strong linear pattern and correlation of 0.99 we are pretty assured this is a good prediction model.

Step 6: Multiple Linear Regression

Sometimes we want to predict something but there is more than one input variable we want to use because the combination of input (x) variables will yield a more refined model. This is called multiple regression. Add to the workflow a second Select Columns widget and set it to have final score as the target (y variable) but leave age, income and hours studied all as features.

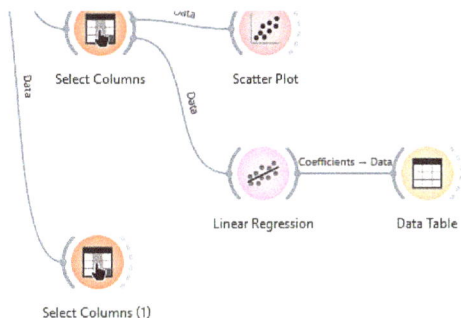

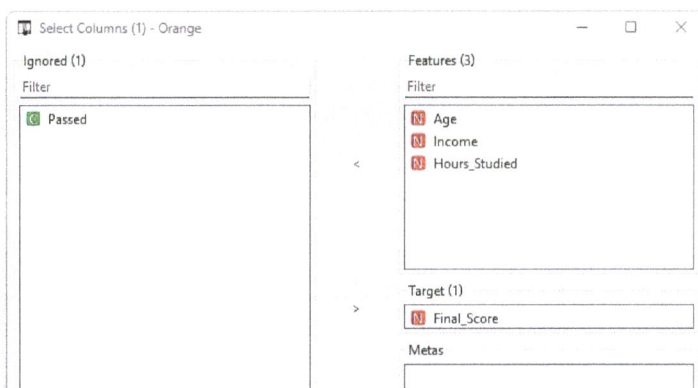

This will allow us to consider the impact of age and income not just hours studied in terms of how they impact the final score. It will produce a model incorporating all three variables. (Optional stop here and view scatterplots of each bivariate relation).

Add to the workflow a second Linear Regression widget and connect it to the new Select Columns widget. Also connect to this a Data Table widget and open it. Make sure the connector says "Coefficients-Data" if not adjust it.

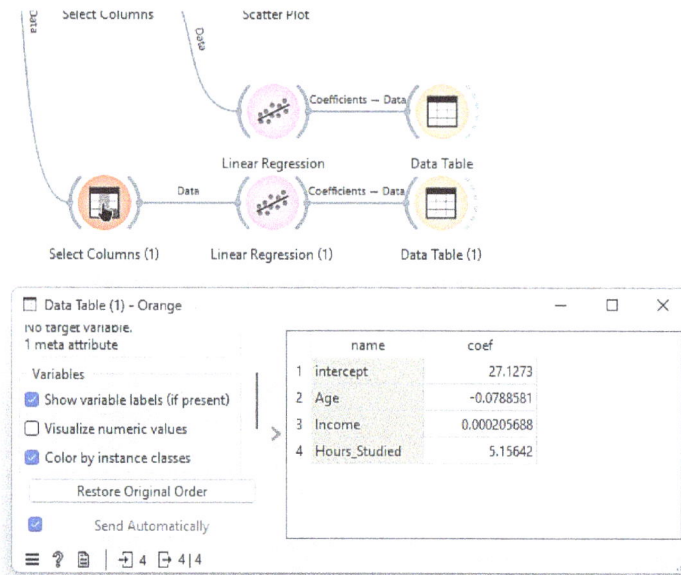

This shows the coefficients for an expanded linear regression where final score can be written as a linear function of age, income and hours studied (y=27.1 + (-0.08*age) + 0 income + 5.16 * hours studied). From this output it is not clear how significant these additional variables are on making a better model (vs the model with just hours studied) and further diagnostics should be done to test this. However, this is more advanced and not optionally done in Orange (would be better done in R or SPSS) so we will not do so here. However, it is informative to know how to make models with multiple input variables.

8.2   Wrap-Up

In this lab, you learned how to build and interpret simple and multiple linear regression models using Orange. By examining both scatterplots and regression outputs, you learned how to mathematically model a relation between two variables with a strong linear relationship. You also got a glimpse of multiple regression which makes models when several factors may influence a result. Linear regression is used for many versatile applications in data analytics.

8.3   Exercises

Linear Regression

For the first dataset, you'll build a simple model using one input to predict an outcome. For the second, you'll expand that to include several input variables.

Use Orange's tools to make scatterplots, check correlations, and run linear regression. Take note of the equations and what the slope and intercept tell you. Then reflect on whether the models seem useful and what the results suggest about each variable's role.

Dataset 1: grades-study.tab

This dataset includes student data such as hours spent studying, number of tutoring sessions, and final exam scores.

1. What does the scatterplot suggest about the relationship between Study-Hours and FinalScore?

2. What is the correlation value shown on the scatterplot?

3. What is the regression equation from the Linear Regression model? Write it in the form y = intercept + slope × StudyHours.

4. What does the slope mean in this context?

5. Based on the scatterplot and correlation, would you trust this regression model for prediction? Why or why not?

Dataset 2: employee-performance.tab

This dataset includes employee information such as hours trained, job satisfaction, age, and performance score.

6. What is the multiple linear regression equation for predicting Performance-Score using HoursTrained, Satisfaction, and Age?

7. Which variable has the strongest effect on PerformanceScore based on the slope value?

8. What does a slope near zero mean in this context, for example with the variable Age?

9. If Satisfaction has a negative slope, what does that suggest? Is it surpris-

ing?

10. Would you keep all three predictors in your model? Why or why not?

Lab 9

Logistic Regression

Linear and logistic regression are both useful tools for making predictions, but they answer different kinds of questions.

Use linear regression when you want to predict a specific number, like a test score. For example, if you know how many hours a student studied, you might use linear regression to estimate their exam score of something like 76 or 89. This method works when the outcome is a continuous value.

On the other hand, logistic regression is better for questions with two possible outcomes, such as pass or fail. Instead of giving you a score, it gives you the likelihood of each outcome. So, if the model predicts a 0.8 (or 80%) chance of passing, you'd likely say the student is predicted to pass. Logistic regression is about predicting categories rather than numbers.

This ability to categorize or classify things is the basis for many important uses in data science and artificial intelligence including being the basis for much of machine learning. There are other classification techniques too, but linear regression is the most foundation conceptual one and builds directly from simple linear regression.

9.1   Lesson Steps

Step 1: Load Data

To load the data in Orange, start Orange and create a new workflow. From the left-hand panel, drag and drop the File widget onto the canvas. Double-click the widget to open it and use the folder icon to browse and load the students.csv file.

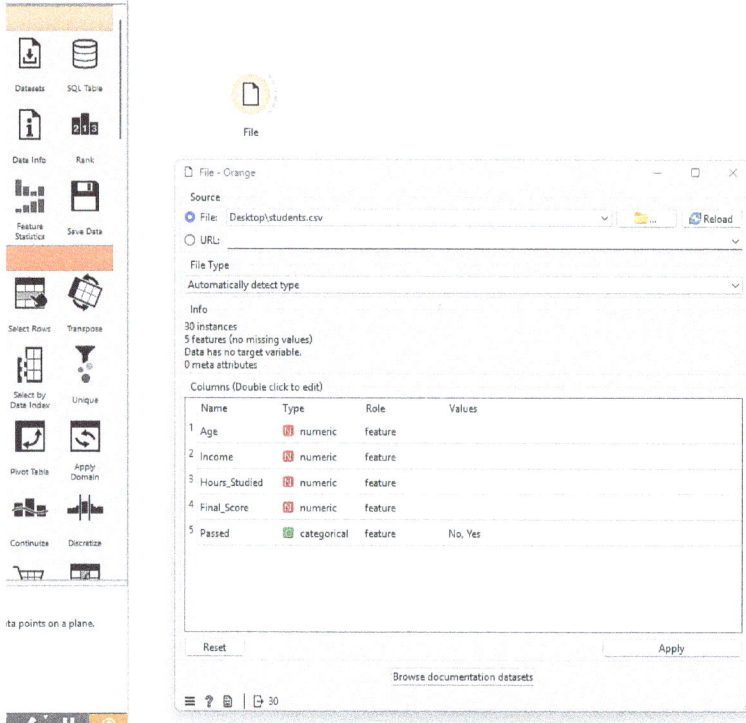

In our data there is a variable 'Passed' – this is a categorical yes or no variable indicating not an actual final score but just the information as to whether the student passed. If this were the only variable we had (and did not have final scores) as an outcome or if we simply wanted to use this instead as out outcome we can use logistic (not linear) regression instead.

Step 2: Look at the Data

Connect to the File widget a Feature Statistics widget to look over the variables and basic statistics on them. (Another option would be to hook up a Data Table and look at that, but Feature Statistics is more useful here).

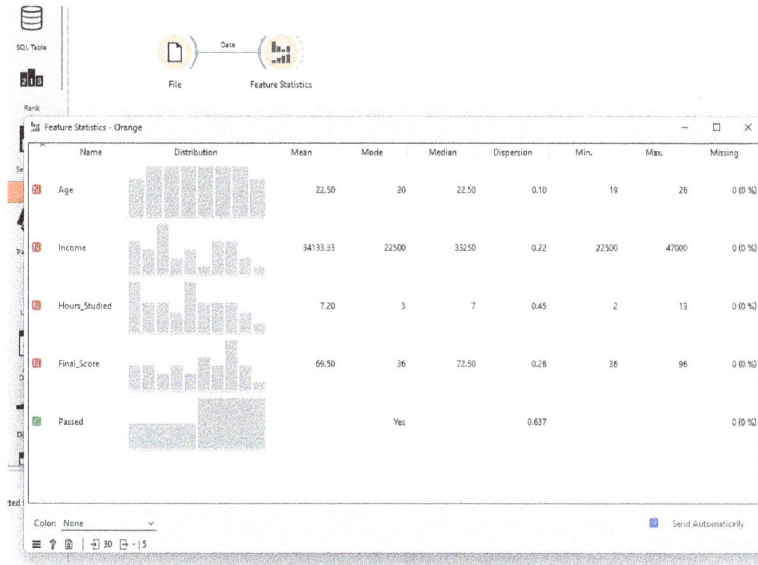

Step 3: Setup Logistic Regression

Add a Select Columns widget to the workflow and set it to have a target of 'Passed' and a feature variable of hours studied (we could do multiple variables as input for a more complex model but will not do so here).

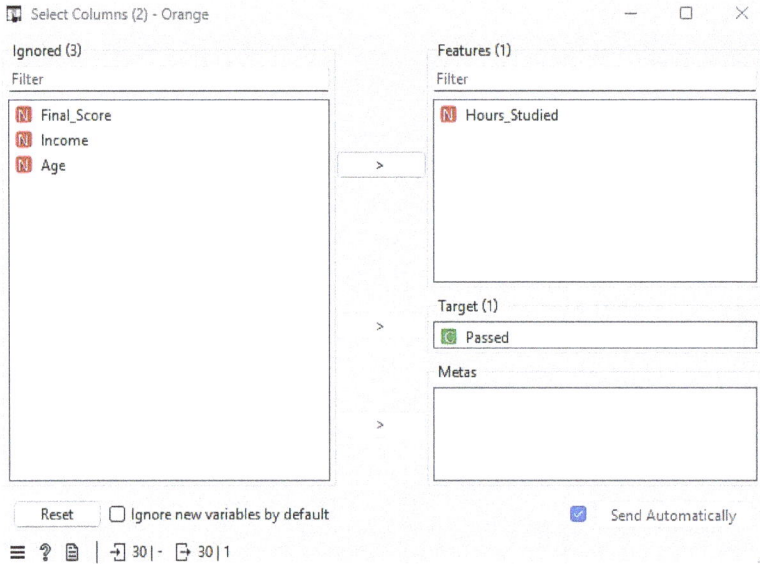

Step 4: Examine Relationship

A great way to look at the relationship of the target variable and input and whether this will be a good model is to first look at a boxplot. Add a Boxplot widget to the workflow and open it.

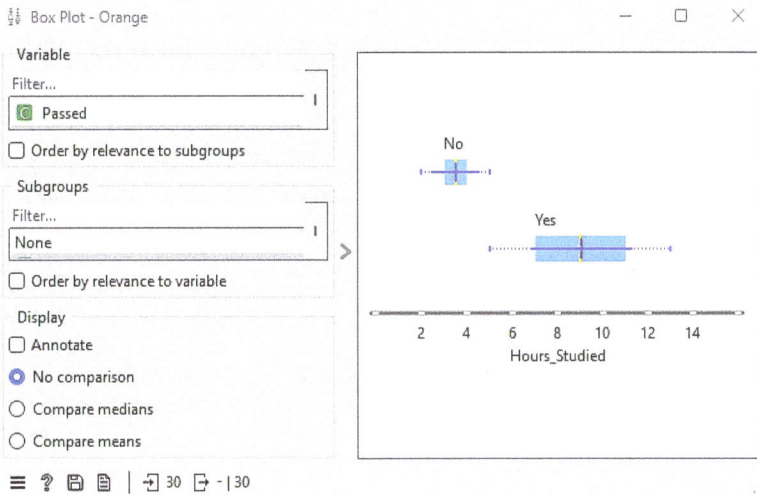

The boxplot shows great separation of the final scores by passed yes or no. You want to see this type of distinction before doing logistic regression. (More sophisticated diagnostics will not be done here but in a more advanced example would be done). Since logistic regression is a classifier model we want to make sure the outcome does nicely separate into categories.

Step 5: Run the Model

Next let's run a logistic regression model. Add to the Select Columns widget a logistic regression widget and add a data table to this. Make sure what flows to the data table is the coefficients labelled on the connector.

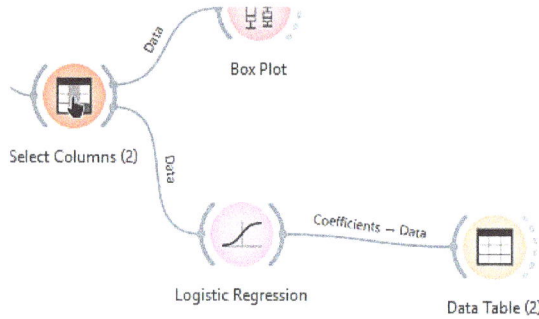

Open the data table.

The output shown includes two important numbers called coefficients: the intercept, which is -8.16987, and the coefficient for Hours_Studied, which is 1.55737. These two values form the equation for the logistic regression model.

Step 6: Interpret the Model

In logistic regression, the model does not predict a score or number directly. Instead, it predicts the probability that the target outcome is "Yes" (in this case, that the student passed).

The model starts by calculating something called the log-odds, which is a special way of expressing probabilities. The formula for this is:

$$\text{Logit}(P) = -8.16987 + 1.55737 \times \text{Hours\_Studied}$$

This means that if a student studied for 0 hours, the log-odds of passing would be just the intercept: -8.16987. This is a very low number, which corresponds to a very small chance of passing. On the other hand, as the number of study hours increases, the log-odds of passing also increase. This is because the coefficient for Hours_Studied is positive (1.55737). A positive coefficient means that more study hours make it more likely the student will pass.

However, since log-odds are not very intuitive to interpret, we usually convert them to probability using a formula called the logistic function. This function transforms the log-odds into a number between 0 and 1, which we can understand as a percentage or chance.

For example, suppose a student studies for 6 hours. First, we calculate the log-odds using the model:

$$\text{Log-odds} = -8.16987 + (1.55737 \times 6) = -8.16987 + 9.34422 = 1.17435$$

Next, we convert the log-odds to a probability:

$$\text{Probability of passing} = \frac{1}{1 + e^{-1.17435}} \approx 0.764$$

This means the model predicts that a student who studies for 6 hours has about a 76.4% chance of passing the exam.

9.2   Wrap-Up

This lab showed how to use logistic regression to predict categorical outcomes like pass or fail, rather than a numerical outcome. You built and interpreted results for a basic logistic model with one input feature. Unlike linear regression, which predicts numbers, logistic regression gives a probability which can be classified. Logistic regression is a useful tool whenever your outcome has two possible categories and is an important technique in data analytics.

9.3 Exercises

Logistic Regression

9.3.1 Directions

Begin by loading the dataset and examining the distribution of the predictor variable across outcome groups using a box plot. Next, build a logistic regression model and note the intercept and coefficient values, which form the equation for log-odds. Use the equation to calculate log-odds for a given predictor value, then convert that to a probability to understand the predicted chance of the outcome.

Dataset 1: prep-course.tab

This dataset includes students' hours spent studying, attendance rate, and whether they passed a preparatory course.

1. Describe the Box Plot that shows the distribution of Hours_Studied by Passed. What does separation tell you?

2. What is the logistic regression equation using the coefficients from the model? Write it in the form: log-odds = intercept + (coefficient × Hours_Studied)

3. Based on your model, what happens to the predicted probability of passing as Hours_Studied increases?

4. What is the predicted log-odds for a student who studied 5 hours?

5. Convert the log-odds from question 4 to a probability using the logistic formula. What is the predicted chance of passing?

Dataset 2: job-offers.tab

This dataset contains job application data including Experience_Years, Has_Degree, and whether the applicant received a job offer.

6. How do the experience levels compare between those who got offers and those who did not? Describe what you see in the Box Plot.

7. What is the logistic regression equation using Experience_Years? Write it in log-odds format.

8. Interpret the coefficient for Experience_Years. What does it suggest about the chance of receiving a job offer?

9. What is the predicted log-odds for someone with 3 years of experience?

10. Convert the log-odds from question 9 to probability. What is their predicted chance of receiving a job offer?

Lab 10

Hypothesis Testing

Hypothesis testing is a statistical method used in data science to decide if there is a real difference between a hypothesized value of something and what the data says. There are many different specific hypothesis tests.

One common test is for a difference between groups to determine if the difference is real ('statistically significant') or just due to random chance. This test, the two-sample independent test on means, compares two groups to see if they are significantly different, for instance, checking if customers from City A spend more than those from City B. The process involves setting a null hypothesis (no difference) and an alternative hypothesis (there is a difference), then using data to see which hypothesis it supports. This is especially useful in data science tasks like A/B testing, customer analysis, or evaluating treatments.

10.1   Lesson Steps

Step 1: Load Data

Open Orange. Drag in a File widget and upload the data tutoring.csv.

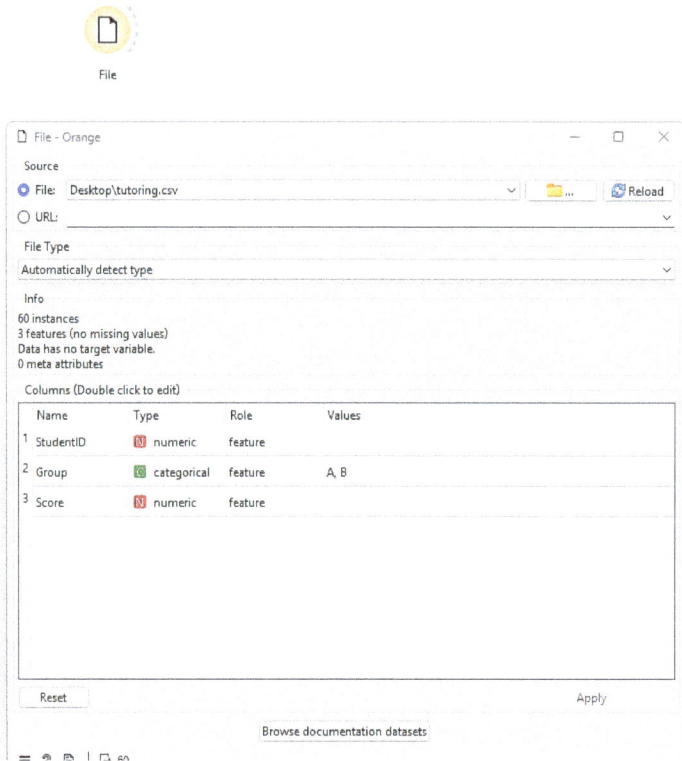

The dataset contains information about 60 students, divided into two groups. Group A includes 30 students who attended tutoring. Group B includes 30 students who did not attend tutoring. Each row in the dataset represents one student and includes three columns: StudentID, Group (A or B), and Score. This dataset has data to use for testing whether tutoring had a significant effect on student performance.

Step 2: Look at Data

Connect a Data Table widget to the File Widget and open it to view the data.

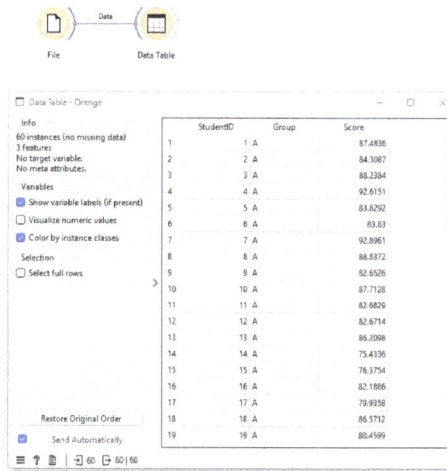

Step 3: Evaluate Group Means

We desire to compare the mean (average) performance of group A (received tutoring) to group B (no tutoring) to determine the effect of tutoring. Let's first look at the means of these by group. To do so connect a Group By widget to the data table and open it. Set it to Group by 'Group' with attribute 'Score' set to show the mean and standard deviation by group.

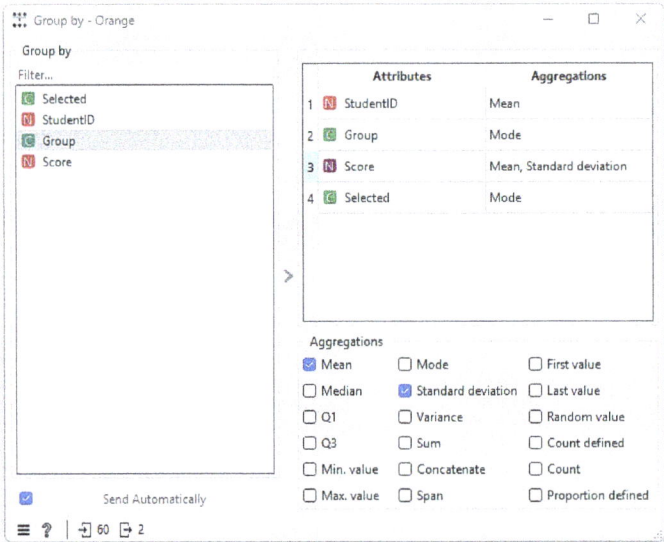

Next add a Data Table widget AFTER the group means, open this and view it.

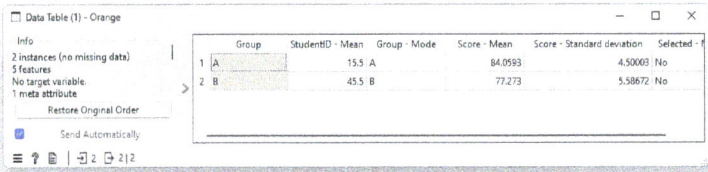

This shows the mean and standard deviation by group for the score variable (it shows other metrics as well, if we wished to we could subset this table to just have the selected results, but we will not need to here – this would be a good idea if for example you were using the result to display in a presentation).

Students who received tutoring (Group A) had an average score of 84.06 with a standard deviation of 4.50, while students who did not receive tutoring (Group B) had a lower average score of 77.27 with a standard deviation of 5.59. This shows a noticeable difference in average performance between the two groups, with Group A scoring about 6.79 points higher on average. However, based on this (because it does not account for variability) we cannot conclude that tutoring caused the improvement just by comparing the means. To determine whether this difference is statistically significant or due to random chance, a two-sample t-test is needed.

Step 4: Boxplot and Hypothesis Test

In Orange, to perform a two independent sample means test use the Box Plot widget. While the box plot is mainly a visualization tool, it also runs a t-test when comparing two groups.

From the original Data Table connect it to the Box Plot widget and set the grouping variable where it says subgroup (e.g., "Group") and the numeric feature variable to compare (e.g., "Score"). Orange will display side-by-side box plots for each group.

To show the test statistics and the p-value from a two-sample t-test below the plot check display and compare means. This allows you to both see and statistically test whether the difference between the two-group means is significant.

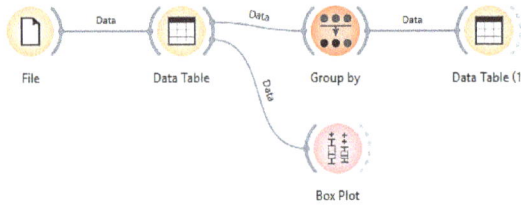

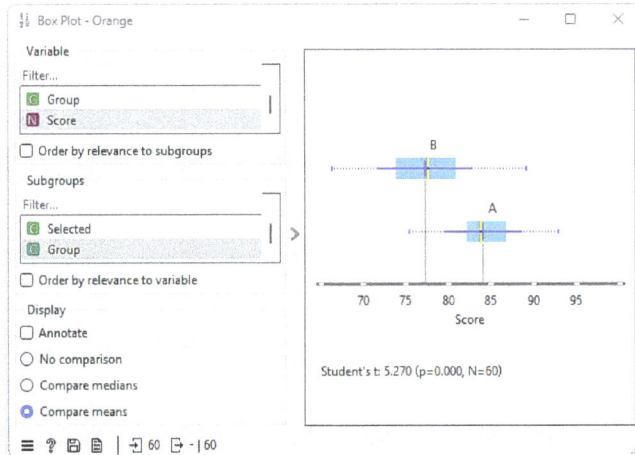

The t-test results show a t-statistic of 5.27 and a p-value of 0 (or effectively 0, meaning $p < 0.001$), with a total sample size of 60 students (30 in each group). This tells us that the difference in average scores between Group A (tutoring) and Group B (no tutoring) is statistically significant. It's very unlikely that this difference happened by chance and we can reject the null hypothesis that there is no difference between the groups.

Since Group A had a higher average score (84.06) compared to Group B (77.27), and the t-test confirms that this difference is real, we can confidently conclude that students who attended tutoring performed significantly better than those who did not.

10.2   Wrap-Up

In this lab, you learned how to use hypothesis testing to determine if the difference between two groups is meaningful or just due to chance. Note that

Orange is not and does not proclaim to be full statistical software and so has limited options for hypothesis testing (unlike R or SPSS software). However basic hypothesis testing helps make informed decisions based on data, which is a key skill in data analysis and real-world problem solving and it is possible to do basic test using Orange.

10.3   Exercises

Comparing Groups with Hypothesis Testing

First, load the data and check the average values in each group. Then, use box plots to get a visual sense of how the groups compare. After that, run a two-sample t-test to see if the difference between the groups is statistically significant. Look at the p-value — if it's low (less than 0.05) that means the difference is probably real, not just chance. Based on what you find, you can decide if there is a statistically significant effect.

Dataset 1: math-review.tab

This dataset contains test scores from students randomly assigned to two groups. Group X attended a math review session before the final exam, and Group Y did not. Each student record includes an ID, the group they belonged to, and their final exam score.

1. What are the mean and standard deviation of scores for each group?

2. What is the difference in mean scores between Group X and Group Y?

3. Describe the Box Plot comparing the two groups. What does the visual suggest about the performance of each group?

4. What is the p-value of the two-sample t-test comparing group scores?

5. Based on the p-value, is the difference statistically significant? What conclusion can you come to?

Dataset 2: reading-hours.tab

This dataset includes weekly reading times for students, along with an indicator of whether they participated in a reading intervention program. The goal is to assess whether the intervention affected reading behavior.

6. What is the average reading time in hours for each group?

7. What is the difference in average reading time between the groups?

8. Describe the Box Plot comparing reading time by group. Do the distributions overlap?

9. What is the t-statistic and p-value shown for the comparison?

10. Do the results support the idea that the intervention increased reading time? Explain using the p-value and group means.

Lab 11

Dealing With Missing Data

Missing data occurs when data entry is incomplete or nonexistent for one or more fields for which there is a record. It is common in real-world datasets and can cause problems in analysis. Problems may include bias (if the missing data is nefarious and due to intentional actions) or the inability to analyze data due to reduced sample size and statistical power. In this exercise, you will explore different approaches for how to deal with missing data so that the data can still be effectively analyzed.

11.1   Lesson Steps

Step 1 Load Data

From the toolbox on the left, drag a File widget into the workflow area. Click on the File widget to open it, then click Browse and select the file named heart_disease_missing.csv from your computer.

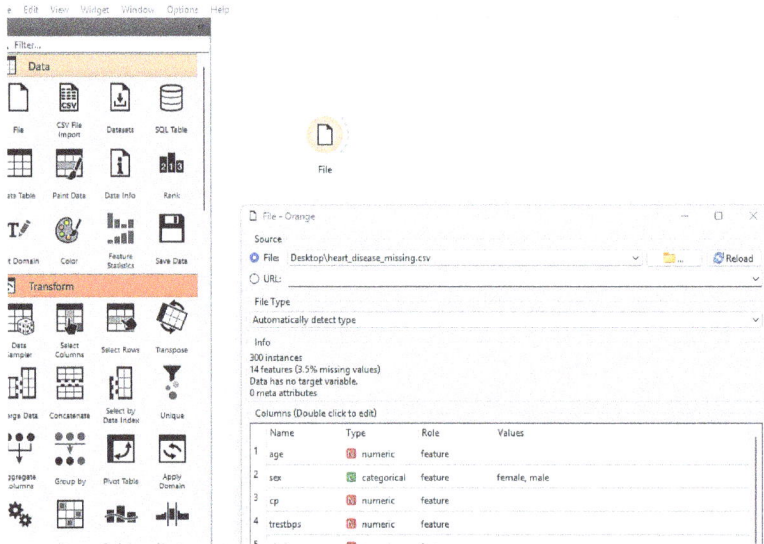

Step 2: View the Data

Add a Data Table widget. Connect the File widget to the Data Table. Open
the Data Table. Note the data has 300 rows.

ige	sex	cp	trestbps	chol	fbs	restecg	thalach	exang	oldpeak
67	female	1	109.6	190.9	0	0	133.9	1	-0.1
57	female	2	166.6	275.8	0	1	182.8	0	1.4
43	female	3	153.6	274.7	0	1	183.6	1	0.8
71	male	0	120.6	229.5	1	1	138.9	1	2.0
36	female	0	95.7	261.3	0	1	161.4	0	2.2
49	male	0	157.1	182.4	0	1	182.6	0	3.6
67	male	2	127.7	291.2	1	0	142.4	0	1.6
47	female	2	154.8	235.8	1	1	145.9	1	1.3
51	male	0	98.1	218.9	1	1	138.4	0	1.2
39	female	3	118.0	297.5	0	0	129.7	1	0.6
39	male	2	130.1	209.8	1	0	137.0	0	1.3
52	female	0	130.9	174.6	1	0	125.5	0	0.7
64	male	0	121.0	167.2	0	1	150.7	1	?
68	female	3	142.5	275.3	1	0	134.6	1	?
52	female	1	108.6	181.0	1	1	154.7	0	-0.0
31	female	2	127.2	332.7	1	1	118.9	1	2.1
50	female	3	132.4	140.9	1	0	156.6	1	2.3
30	female	0	140.3	329.8	0	0	166.7	1	0.9
52	male	0	144.2	?	1	1	110.1	1	-1.1
72	male	3	107.5	240.2	1	0	157.5	1	0.4
58	male	2	99.3	217.8	0	1	174.6	0	2.3
66	female	1	155.6	265.0	1	0	125.8	0	1.0

The data has many places where ? is in the data. Orange puts ? in where data is missing. When you load a CSV file into Orange, any cell that contains a ? is automatically treated as a missing value. You can see these missing values displayed as ? in the Data Table widget.

Step 3: Assess Missing Values

Add a Feature Statistics widget to the workflow and connect it to the Data Table. The Feature Statistics widget in Orange shows the percentage of missing values for each feature, helping you quickly identify columns with incomplete data.

Open the Feature Statistics widget and scroll the data to view how much data is missing.

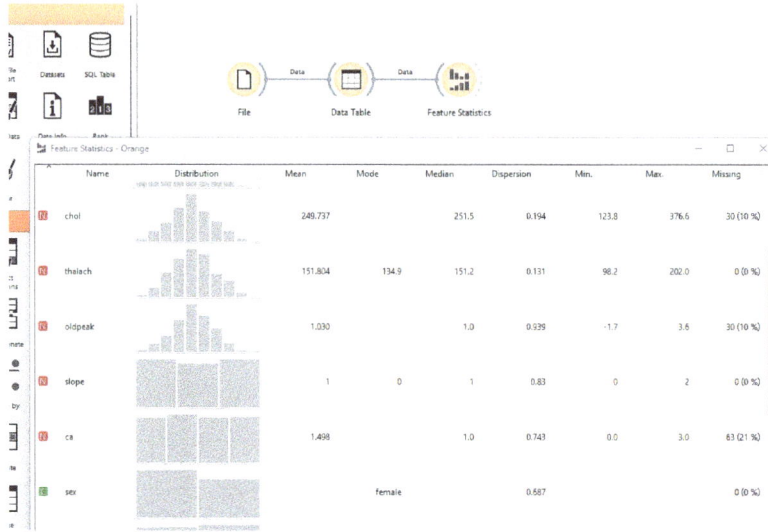

A lot of variables are complete however some of the data such as chol, thalach and ca have 10% more missing data. This could be a problem for analysis.

Step 4: Selective Removal

The easiest way to deal with missing data is to simply remove those records from the dataset. If for example cholesterol were missing and a necessary variable for the analysis being done (such that having missing values would prevent successful analysis) simply removing those rows may work as an option. There are many problems with this – such as it reducing sample size (especially if there are a lot of missing's), creating bias in the data (if the missing's were not at random) and that data with removed values is always suspect.

Let's add a Select Rows widget to the workflow and connect it to the Data Table. Select Rows is used to filter or remove entire rows (data entries). You can tell it to remove rows where a certain value is missing (like if chol is not defined) or keep only rows that meet a condition (like age > 50). This is useful when you want to focus on complete or relevant records and ignore rows that are incomplete. Open the widget and set it to chol is defined as a row selection filter.

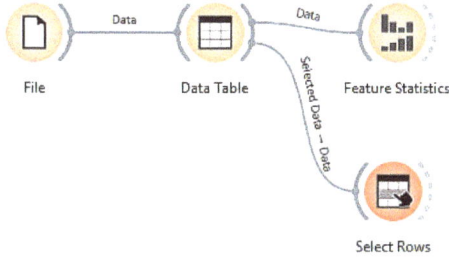

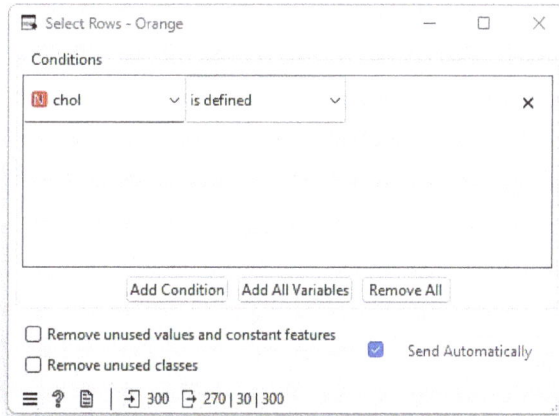

Add a Data Table AFTER the select rows and then a Feature Statistics widget after this. Open the Feature Statistics widget and look at the chol data. You will now see it has 0% missing values. The data now has 270 rows (of the original 300) as the 30 rows with missing data were removed. In these rows of course much of the rest of the data for other variables was there (as we were filtering for missing chol only) so that data is now removed.

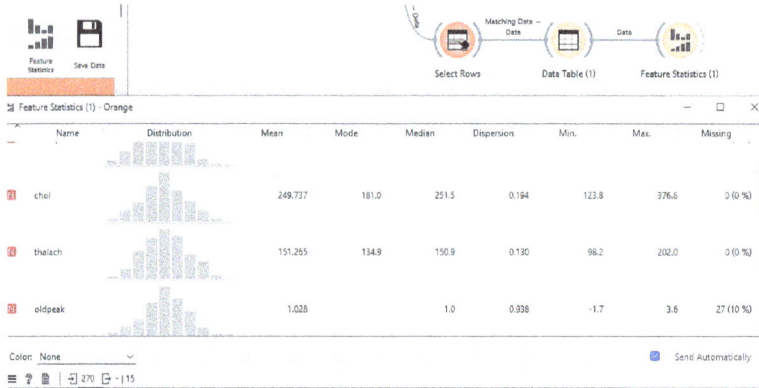

Step 5: Remove All Missing Data

If you needed every value of every variable to be non-missing you could take the (somewhat drastic) step of cleaning the data to remove EVERY row containing any missing data value in any of the features.

To do this add a preprocess widget to the workflow connected to the original data table. Set the preprocess widget as depicted below with Remove Sparse Features as the selected preprocessor and on the right for the specifics of Impute Missing values select Remove rows with missing values (if there are other things on the right side remove them using the upper right x on the selection – Orange may have default settings applied you don't need).

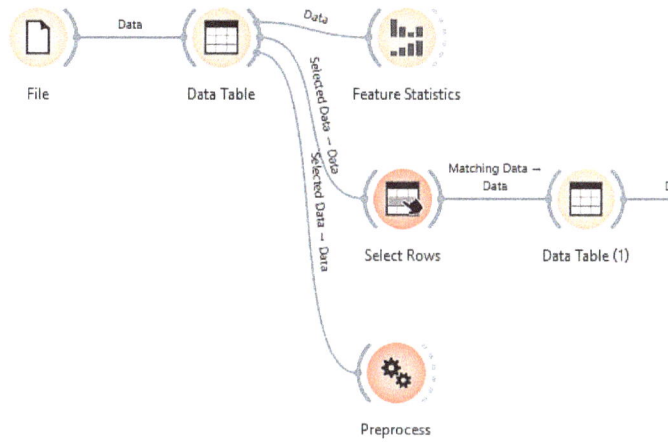

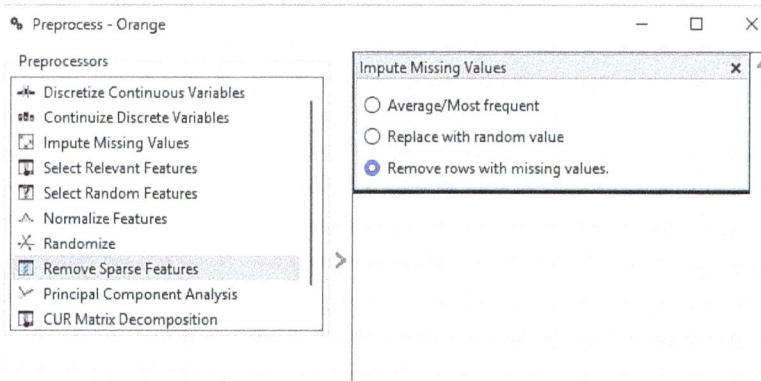

Add to the workflow a new Data Table and connect it to the Preprocess widget.

Open the data table. You will now see it has 179 rows (of the original 300). Although the missing data has been removed so has a substantive amount of the original data. And you now have only 2/3 of the records in your sample size to work with. You may have deleted records because they had data missing in fields you didn't even need in your analysis.

Step 6: Imputation

Rather than delete rows with missing data a better option may be imputation. Imputation is the process of filling in missing values with estimated ('imputed') values. Instead of deleting rows or columns that have missing data, imputation allows you to keep more of your data records. This is especially useful when many rows contain some missing values and removing them would result in much smaller sample sizes.

Imputation is also often better than deletion because it helps avoid bias. If the missing data is not random—for example, if certain groups are more likely to have missing values—deleting those rows can distort your results. Imputation also helps preserve the patterns and structure of the dataset by using logical estimates, such as the mean, median, or predicted values based on other variables.

There are different methods of imputation. One common method of imputation is to replace missing values with the mean or median of that column. This works well for numerical data and helps keep the overall shape of the data. For categorical data, you can use the most frequent value (mode) to fill in blanks. Another option is predictive imputation, where a model (like k-nearest neighbors or regression) estimates the missing values based on other available information.

Let's use imputation with the most common value here. Add a second preprocess widget connected to the original data. Set this to do Average/most frequent for the imputation method.

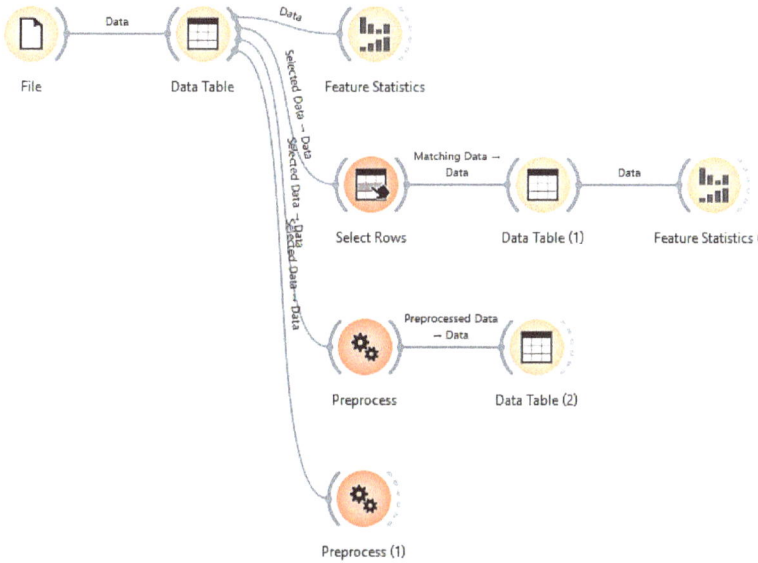

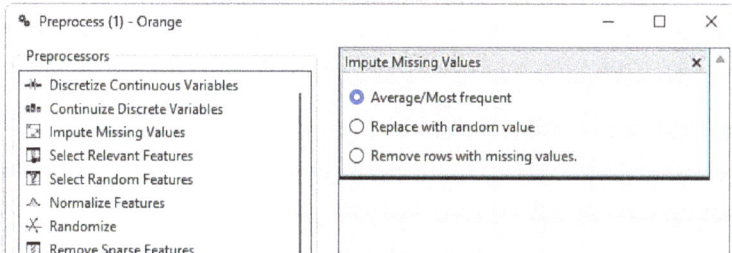

Orange senses the data type and if the data is categorical does imputation with the mode. If the data is quantitative it will do imputation with a numeric average.

Connect a data table to the preprocess widget and open it.

The final data has all 300 rows values that have been filled in with averages for that variable where the values were missing. For example, several chol values are 249.737 the average of that measure.

11.2   Wrap-Up

Handling missing data is a crucial step in preparing datasets for analysis. In this lab, you explored several ways to address missing values using Orange. You learned how to inspect your data for missing entries, remove rows selectively, drop all incomplete rows, and apply imputation techniques to fill in missing values. While removing data can sometimes be necessary, it often leads to smaller or biased datasets. Imputation offers a useful alternative that allows you to keep more data intact by estimating the missing values. Choosing the right strategy depends on the context of your analysis. Knowing how to apply each method gives you the tools to manage missing data effectively and keep your analysis reliable.

11.3   Exercises

Missing Data

Dataset 1: patients_missing.tab
This dataset contains basic medical data for 50 patients, with some missing values in cholesterol, heart rate, and exercise status.

Load `patients_missing.tab` in Orange using the File widget.Connect a Data Table and inspect the data.. Add a Feature Statistics widget to check the percentage of missing values per column.

1. How many rows are in the original dataset?

2. Which variable(s) have missing data, and what is the percentage missing for each?

3. Use a Select Rows widget to remove rows where cholesterol (`chol`) is missing. How many rows are left afterward?

4. Does the percentage of missing values for `chol` become 0 after filtering?

5. What are some limitations of simply removing rows with missing data?

6. Add a Preprocess widget and set it to remove all rows with any missing value. How many rows remain now?

7. How many rows were deleted in total by this method?

8. When might you want to avoid this approach?

9. Create a second Preprocess widget and set it to use "Average/Most Frequent" imputation. What happens to the missing values?

10. What imputed value appears for missing `chol` entries?

11. How does imputation help preserve sample size compared to deletion?

12. What is one potential downside of imputation using the average?

Dataset 2: student_scores_missing.tab
This dataset contains test scores, hours studied, and whether students passed, but with several missing entries.

Load `student_scores_missing.tab` using the File widget. Use Feature Statistics to inspect missingness. Try both row deletion and imputation methods using Preprocess widgets.

Questions

13. How many rows are deleted when removing any row with missing data?

14. What is the imputed value used for missing `Hours_Studied`?

15. Compare the final row counts for deletion vs. imputation. Which method retains more data?

Lab 12

Data Wrangling Basics

In most real-world projects, raw data is rarely ready for analysis straight out of the box. It usually needs to be cleaned, filtered, or reshaped. Data wrangling is the process of preparing data for analytics.

In this lab, you'll learn how to carry out basic wrangling tasks. These include viewing the data, filtering specific rows, selecting certain columns, and creating summary statistics through grouping. Each of these steps play an important role in helping you prepare your data for analysis or visualization.

12.1   Lesson Steps

Step 1 Load Data

Open new Orange workflow, add a File widget and upload the 'penquins.csv' dataset.

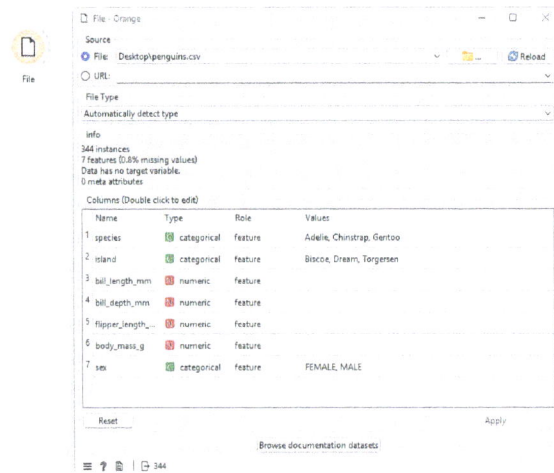

The penguin data is a dataset with measurements of three penguin species—Adélie, Chinstrap, and Gentoo—collected from islands near Antarctica. It includes information like bill length and depth, flipper length, body mass, species type, island location, sex, and the year the data was collected. This dataset is often used to practice data analysis and machine learning because it's simple, clean, and has both numeric and categorical variables.

Step 2 View Data

Connect the File widget to a new Data Table widget. Open this and view the data

Step 3 Subset Data - Rows

The purpose of subsetting data is to focus on a smaller part of the dataset that meets certain conditions. This helps you analyze or work with only the relevant data you need. Also, if the data is large it is often easier to work with a smaller subset of the data.

In Orange, the Select Rows widget lets you choose specific rows based on rules or filters you set. For example, you might select only rows where a value is greater than a number or where a category matches something. This is a way to filter the dataset to keep only rows you want.

Add a Select Rows widget to the workflow. Connect this to the data table and open it. Set it to the condition species is Adelie.

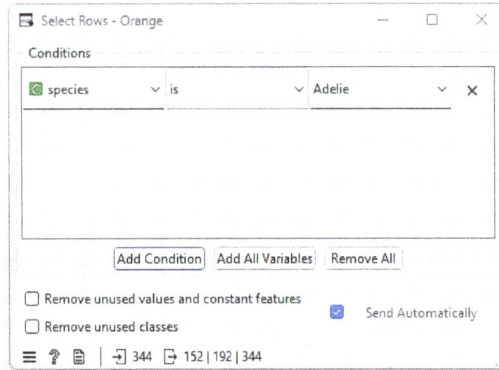

Add a data table to this and open it to view. The data is now subsetted and the new Data Table contains only Adelie species of penguins. This would enable a researcher to focus only on the data of interest if they were only studying this species.

	Selected	species	island	bill_length_mm	bill_depth_mm	lipp
1	No	Adelie	Torgersen	39.1	18.7	
2	No	Adelie	Torgersen	39.5	17.4	
3	No	Adelie	Torgersen	40.3	18.0	
4	No	Adelie	Torgersen	?	?	
5	No	Adelie	Torgersen	36.7	19.3	
6	No	Adelie	Torgersen	39.3	20.6	
7	No	Adelie	Torgersen	38.9	17.8	
8	No	Adelie	Torgersen	39.2	19.6	
9	No	Adelie	Torgersen	34.1	18.1	
10	No	Adelie	Torgersen	42.0	20.2	
11	No	Adelie	Torgersen	37.8	17.1	
12	No	Adelie	Torgersen	37.8	17.3	
13	No	Adelie	Torgersen	41.1	17.6	
14	No	Adelie	Torgersen	38.6	21.2	
15	No	Adelie	Torgersen	34.6	21.1	

Info: 152 instances, 7 features (0.9 % missing data), Target with 2 values, No meta attributes.

Step 4 Subset Data - Columns

Another way to work with a smaller dataset with more specific criteria is to select only certain variables (features) and create a dataset with fewer columns although retaining all the rows. Again, this would create a smaller and often more manageable dataset to work with.

Add a Select Columns widget to the workflow and connect it to the original Data Table. Open it. Let's say we are just studying bill (of the Penguin) measurements and the species. Leave under feature the bill_length and bill_depth and species features and put the rest of the features under ignore.

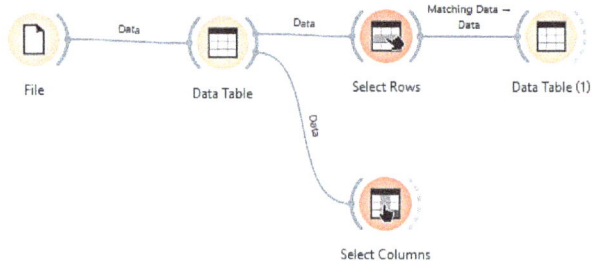

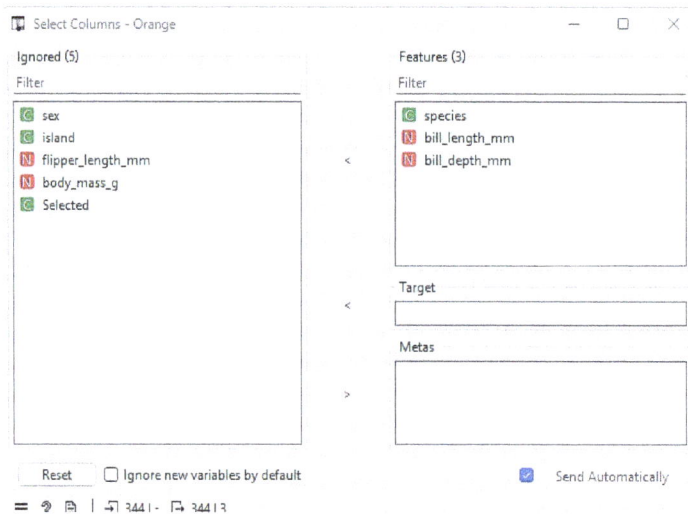

Add a new Data Table widget and connect it to the Select Columns widget.

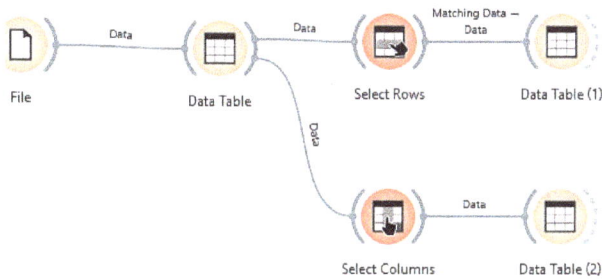

Open this and see that the data now only has the three selected columns.

Step 5 Aggregate data

Creating aggregates from raw data is important because it helps simplify and summarize large, detailed datasets into more manageable and meaningful information. Raw data often contains many individual records with lots of details, which can be overwhelming and noisy. By aggregating—like calculating averages, sums, counts, or totals—you can reveal patterns, trends, or overall insights that are harder to see at the raw level.

Aggregate data is commonly used for graphs and presenting results. Generally, when doing basic analytics, you use the non-aggregated data for modelling and testing and descriptive statistics.

Let's aggregate as an example the body mass of Penguins by species. Connect to the original data table a Group by widget (under the transform menu, note this is not the Aggregate columns widget which we will not be using). To group the data by species, go to the left pane under "Group by" and select species. This tells Orange to summarize the data so that each row in the output corresponds to a different penguin species.

Next, choose the attribute you want to calculate the mean for. In the middle pane labeled Attributes, make sure body_mass_g is checked. Then, in the right column under Aggregations, select Mean as the aggregation function for body_mass_g. (In your screenshot, this is already correctly set.)

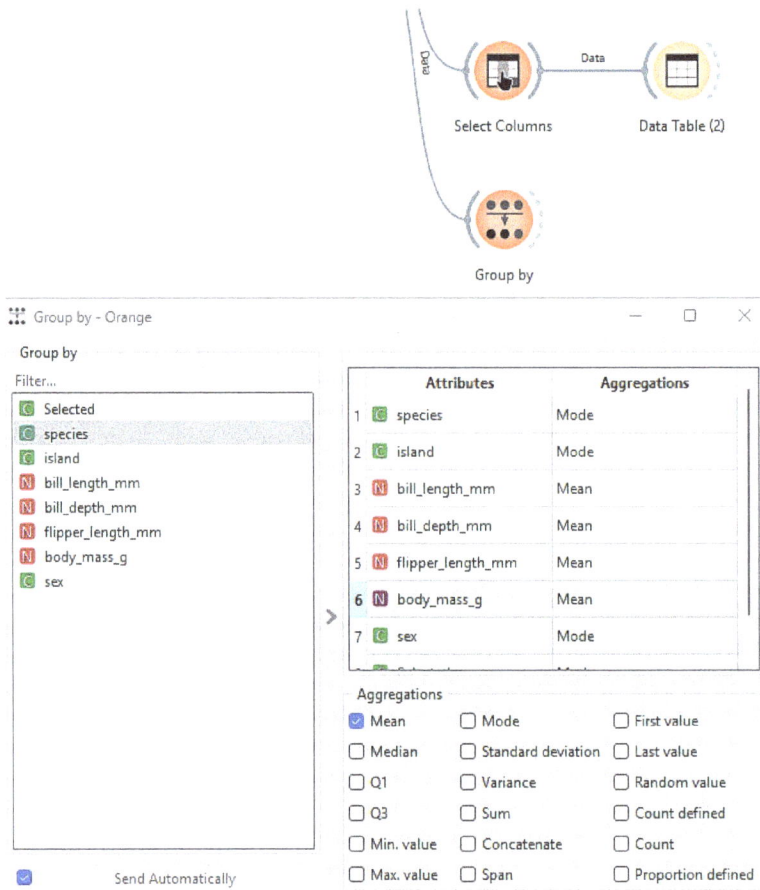

Connect the Group by widget to a new Data Table and open it. Note it has all the variables in it (with means and modes). If you don't want all this, for example, for using it as a display table then you can use the Select Columns widget to filter it out.

However, to use this aggregated data for a plot, for example there is no need to remove the other columns. Connect a Bar plot widget to the aggregate data table result. Open this and set values to the body mass variable and color by species.

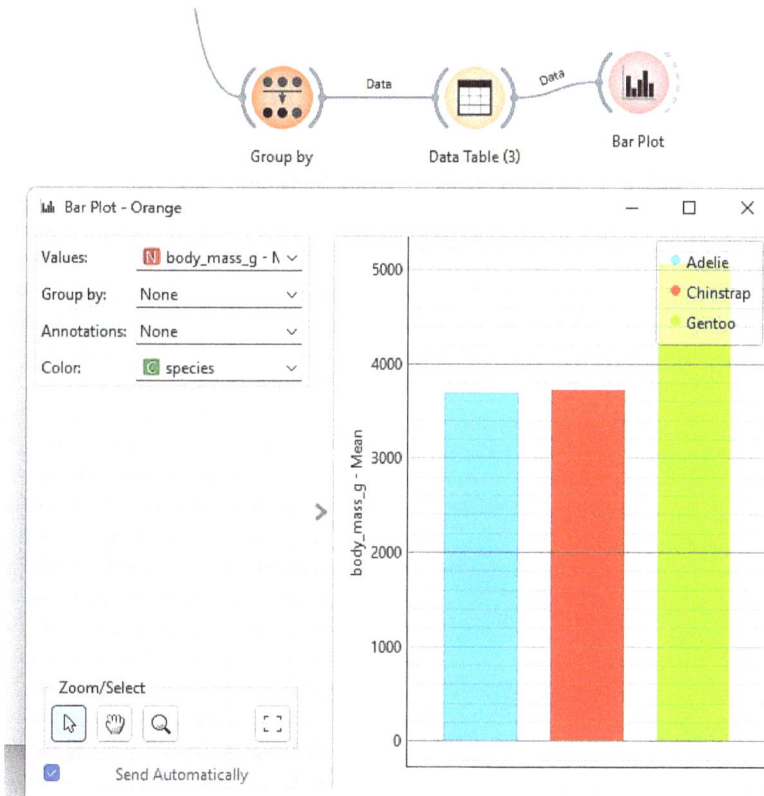

We now have an informative graph of the mean body mass by species.

12.2   Wrap-Up

In this lab, you explored some of the most important data wrangling techniques. You practiced filtering rows based on specific conditions, selecting only certain features to include in your analysis, and summarizing data using grouping and aggregation. These steps help turn raw data into something more structured, focused, and easier to analyze or visualize. Wrangling is a key part of the data analysis process—whether you're building models or creating reports, being able to shape your dataset into the right form makes everything else smoother and more effective.

12.3 Exercises

Data Wrangling Basics

Start a new Orange workflow and add a File widget. Load the dataset named car_sales.csv. Connect the File widget to a Data Table widget and open it to view the dataset.

Next, add a Select Rows widget to filter for cars where the price is greater than 25000. Connect this to a Data Table to see how many cars meet this condition. Then, add another Select Rows widget after the first one and set it to include only rows where the status is "sold". Open the connected Data Table to view how many sold cars priced above 25000 remain and which car makes are present.

To reduce the number of columns, add a Select Columns widget and choose to keep only the make, price, and mileage columns. Connect this to a Data Table and check how many columns remain.

To calculate average values, add a Group By widget. Set it to group the data by make, then select price and mileage under attributes and set the aggregation function for both to Mean. Connect the Group By widget to a Data Table to view the average price and mileage for each car make.

Use this information to answer the exercise questions and understand how filtering, selecting, and aggregating help organize data for analysis.

Dataset: car_sales.csv

1. How many cars have a price above $25,000?

2. After filtering cars priced above $25,000, how many entries remain?

3. Which car makes are represented in the filtered dataset?

4. After selecting columns, how many columns does the dataset have?

5. What is the average price and mileage for each car make?

6. Which car make has the highest average price?

7. Why might filtering by sold cars and price be useful for a sales analysis?

8. How could selecting specific columns help in speeding up analysis?

9. If you wanted to analyze unsold cars only, how would you change the workflow?

10. What other aggregation functions could be useful besides mean?

Lab 13

Cluster Analysis

Clustering is a type of machine learning used to group data based on patterns, without needing labels or predefined categories. Basically, clustering looks for natural similarities among the data points (using mathematical distances) and organizes them into groups. This approach is useful when you're trying to uncover hidden patterns—for example, finding groups of customers who shop in similar ways or sorting documents by topic.

A popular method for clustering is called K-Means. With this method, you choose how many groups (K) you want to cluster (based on variance analysis, coverage of which is beyond the scope here). The clustering algorithm works to divide the data into that many clusters. It does this by measuring how close each point is to the center of a group, known as the centroid. Points are assigned to the group whose centroid they are nearest to. Then, the centroids are updated, and the process repeats until the groupings settle. The goal is to form clear and meaningful clusters of data that are related that can help reveal structure and trends within the data.

13.1   Lesson Steps

Step 1 Load Data

Open a new Orange workflow and add a File widget. Upload the 'health.csv' data. Adjust the role of PatientID to skip (this is just an identifier, and we don't want it in our cluster analysis) and the type to text.

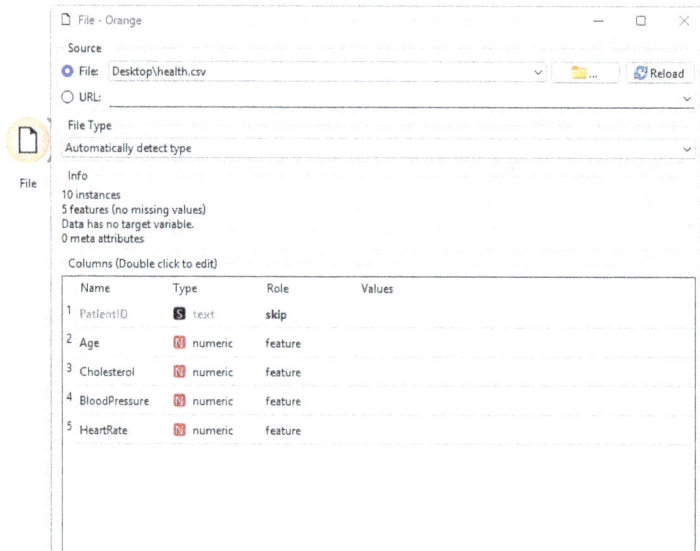

Connect this to a Data Table and open this data to view.

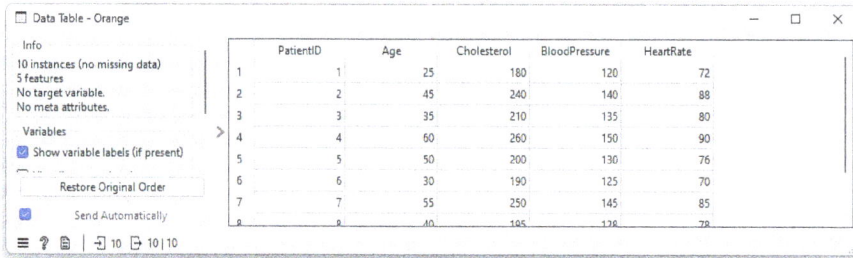

This dataset provides basic health information for ten individual patients. Each row represents one patient and includes details such as their age, cholesterol level, blood pressure, and heart rate. The PatientID serves as a unique identifier for each person. Age ranges from 25 to 65 years, giving a mix of younger and older adults. Cholesterol levels vary from 180 to 270 mg/dL, with higher numbers potentially indicating greater risk for heart disease. BloodPressure values range from 118 to 160, representing systolic blood pressure levels, where higher values may signal hypertension. Lastly, HeartRate is given in beats per minute, ranging from 68 to 95. This kind of dataset is useful for analyzing health patterns and could be used in clustering tasks to group patients with similar health characteristics.

Step 2 Normalize the Data

Add a Preprocess widget (from the Transform menu) to the workflow and connect it to the Data Table. Open the Preprocess widget and set it to (on the right side) Normalize and the option standardize to mean 0, variance 1 (the standard normal score normalization).

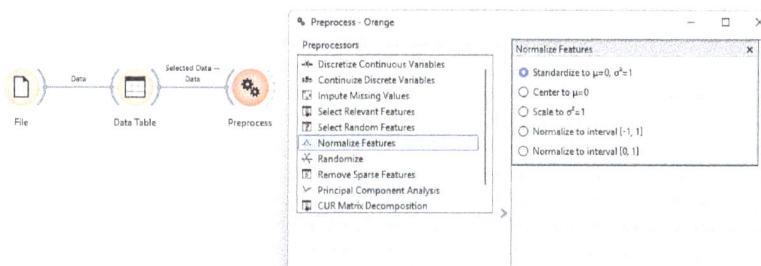

In this Step , you're preparing the data for clustering by making sure all features are on the same scale. You do this by adding the Normalize widget in Orange and connecting it to your dataset. Inside the widget, you select "Normalize by Z-score", which adjusts each feature so that it has a mean of 0 and a standard deviation of 1.

This is important because features like Cholesterol, which has values around 200, could dominate the clustering process over smaller-scale features like Age (30–60) or HeartRate (70–90). By normalizing to standard z scores, each feature contributes equally to the distance calculations that the clustering algorithm uses. The result is more balanced and meaningful clusters.

Add a Data Table widget to the Preprocess widget and open it to view the normalized data. This data can now be used for clustering.

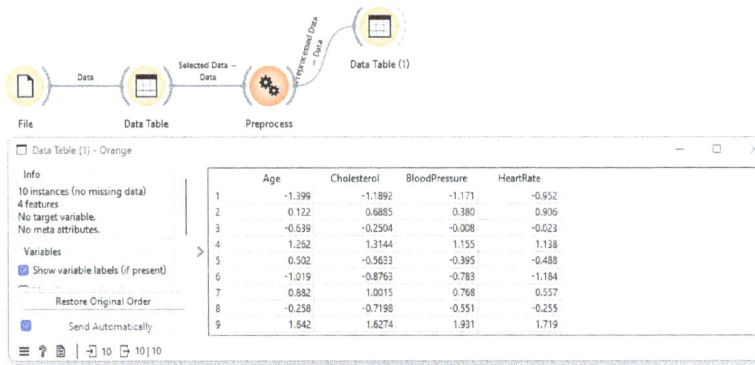

Step 3 K-Means Clustering

Let's run the k means clustering algorithm. Running the K-Means clustering algorithm groups the data into a set number of clusters based on feature similarity (mathematical distances). It assigns each data point to the nearest cluster center (centroid) and updates the centers until the groups are well-formed. This helps reveal patterns or groupings in the data without needing labels. The mathematics of this we will not go into detail but essentially it is figuring out distance wise which points are closer to each other.

Add a K Means widget (from the Unsupervised menu, for unsupervised learning like clustering that has no label) to the workflow and connect it to the Data Table with the normalized data via the Preprocess widget. Open it and set the number of clusters to 3 (K means needs to know this beforehand, the details of how this is determined are beyond the scope of this lesson but 3 is a good number of clusters to assume here).

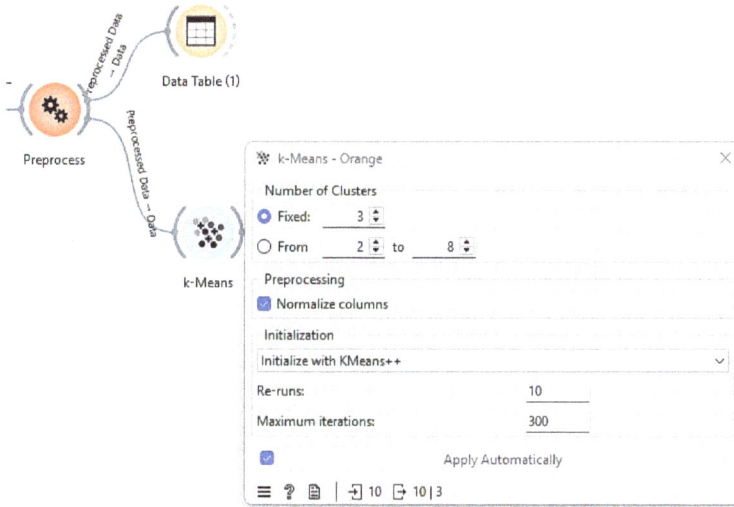

Step 4: View the Clusters

The clusters can be viewed in a new data table or (more interestingly) graphically. To view the clusters in a data table, connect a Data Table widget to the K Means widget. Open this and view the data. Each data point is now assigned to one of 3 clusters (C1 to C3)

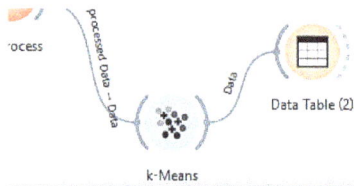

Data Table (2) - Orange

	Cluster	Silhouette	Age	Cholesterol	BloodPressure	HeartRate
1	C1	0.686695	-1.399	-1.1892	-1.171	-0.952
2	C2	0.539404	0.122	0.6885	0.380	0.906
3	C3	0.626443	-0.639	-0.2504	-0.008	-0.023
4	C2	0.678592	1.262	1.3144	1.155	1.138
5	C3	0.639118	0.502	-0.5633	-0.395	-0.488
6	C1	0.666622	-1.019	-0.8763	-0.783	-1.184
7	C2	0.639	0.882	1.0015	0.768	0.557
8	C3	0.630743	-0.258	-0.7198	-0.551	-0.255
9	C2	0.661243	1.642	1.6274	1.931	1.719
10	C1	0.692606	-1.095	-1.0328	-1.326	-1.417

Another way to view the clusters is with a scatterplot where we can see where the clusters are visually. Add a Scatter plot widget to the workflow and connect it to the K Means widget. Within the scatter plot, set the X-axis to Cholesterol and the Y-axis to Blood Pressure so you can visually compare these two important health features. Set the color attribute to 'Cluster' and the 3 clusters are apparent.

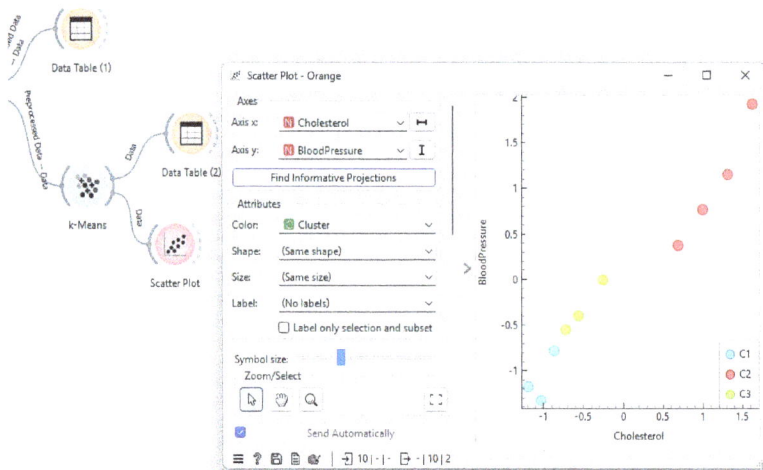

The final clusters are groups of patients that the K-Means algorithm creates based on how similar their health data is. After the computer looks at features like age, cholesterol, blood pressure, and heart rate (all adjusted equally because of normalization), it puts patients into clusters. For example, one cluster might have younger patients with lower cholesterol and blood pressure, another cluster might have patients with average levels, and the last cluster might have older patients with higher cholesterol and blood pressure. You can see which patient is in which cluster in the labelled data table created after running K-Means.

13.2   Wrap-Up

In this lab, you used clustering to explore patterns in a small health dataset. You started by loading and inspecting the data, then prepared it for analysis by normalizing the features to ensure fair comparisons across different scales. Using the K-Means algorithm, you grouped patients into three clusters based on similarities in their health measurements. Finally, you viewed the cluster assignments in a table and used a scatter plot to visualize how the groups differed, particularly by cholesterol and blood pressure. Clustering can reveal meaningful patterns in data even when no labels are provided. After clustering you can create labels like 'cluster 1 young and healthy', etc. based on the clusters. This then allows us to use supervised machine learning techniques (which need labelled data). Clustering is a powerful tool for exploring and organizing complex information.

13.3   Exercises

K-Means Clustering

Load the dataset using the File widget and view it in a Data Table. Skip any ID columns that are not needed for analysis.

Add a Preprocess widget and normalize the numeric features to prepare the data for clustering.

Use the K Means widget to run clustering. Set the number of clusters as needed.

Connect a Data Table to view the cluster assignments.

Add a Scatter Plot to visualize how the clusters are grouped using two selected features, and color the points by cluster.

Use the information in the output and cluster centroids to answer questions about group size, feature values, and differences between clusters.

Dataset 1: Customer Purchase Behavior

Dataset: customer_data.csv

1. Load the data and view it. How many features (columns) are there excluding CustomerID?

2. Normalize the data (Age, Income, Spending Score) before clustering. What is the mean and standard deviation of the normalized Annual Income column?

3. Run K-Means clustering with K=3. How many customers belong to cluster 2?

4. After clustering, create a scatter plot with X = Annual Income and Y = Spending Score. How are the clusters visually separated?

5. Based on the cluster centroids, describe the characteristics (age and spending) of cluster 1.

Dataset 2: Vehicle Specifications

Dataset: vehicle_data.csv

6. Load and view the dataset. How many vehicles have an engine size larger than 3.0 liters?

7. Normalize all numeric features (Engine Size, Horsepower, Weight, Acceleration). What is the normalized value of the vehicle with the largest weight?

8. Perform K-Means clustering with K=2. How many vehicles are assigned to cluster 1?

9. Create a scatter plot of Horsepower vs Acceleration, colored by cluster assignment. Describe the main difference between the two clusters.

10. Based on the cluster centroids, which cluster tends to have faster acceleration times and heavier vehicles?

Lab 14

Classification Analysis

Classification is a type of supervised machine learning used to automatically assign items into categories based on their features (aka labels, classifiers). It's widely used in many fields—like predicting whether a customer will churn, detecting spam emails, diagnosing diseases, or sorting images. The goal of this 'supervised' learning is to learn patterns from labeled examples so the model can accurately predict the category (label) of new, unseen data.

14.1 Lesson Steps

Step 1 Load Data

Open a new workflow and add a File widget to the workflow. Open the file widget and load the data 'churn.csv'.

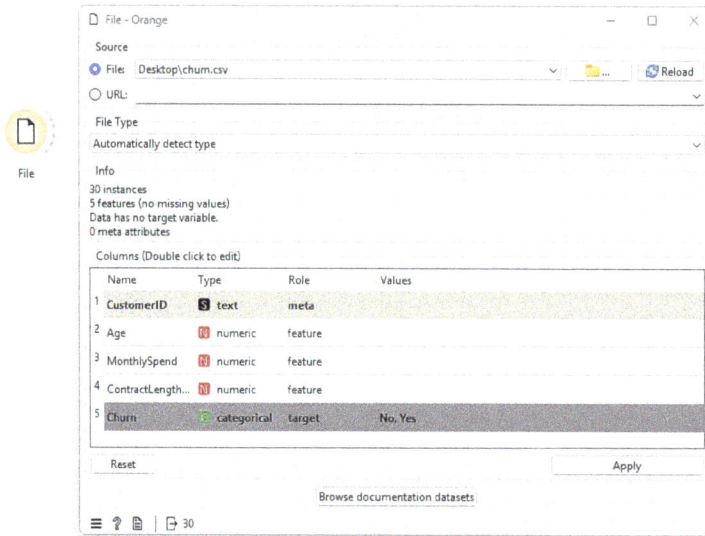

Set churn to the target variable and make sure it is of categorical type (it is the label for supervised learning). Set CustomerID to text and meta (it is not to be used as an input feature in the model).

This dataset contains basic customer information to analyze churn behavior, including customer ID, age, monthly spending, contract length in months, and whether the customer churned (Yes or No). The dataset's features like Age, MonthlySpend, and ContractLengthMonths are numeric, while Churn is the target categorical variable (feature), making it suitable for supervised learning tasks in Orange. Supervised learning MUST have a categorical label variable to use.

Step 2 View Data

Add a Data Table widget and open it to view the data after connecting it to the file widget.

Step 3 Create Train and Test Subsets

The Data Sampler widget in Orange splits a dataset into two parts— a training set from which the model is built and a test set with which the model is evaluated. For example, it might take 70% of the data for training the model and keep 30% aside to test how well the model performs on new, unseen data.

Splitting the data ensures that you don't just train and evaluate your model on the same data. If you tested the same data you trained on, the model could just memorize it, giving an overly optimistic view of its accuracy. By holding out a separate test set, you get a realistic measure of how well the model will perform in real-world situations on data it hasn't seen before.

Add a Data Sampler widget (from the Transform menu) to the workflow by connecting it to the data table. Open this and set it to sample 70% of the data – this we will use to make the model. The reserve 30% we will use for testing how good the model is (with a data set of n=30 samples a 70/30 split like this gives 9 values to test – with larger data typically 80/20 would be used but with this data this would only give 6 to test so using 70/30 is a better option).

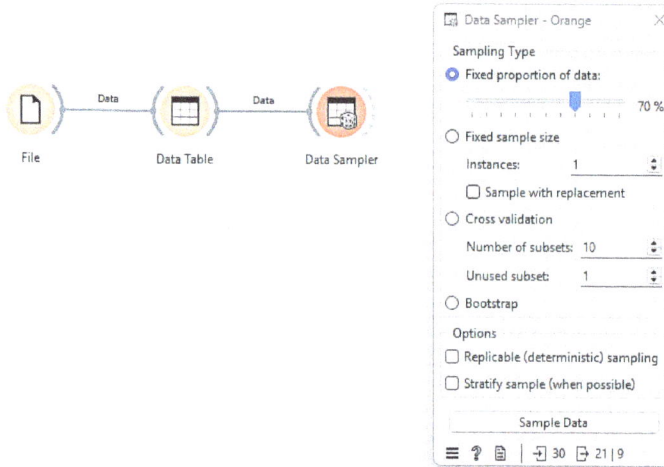

Step 4 Setup the Model

We have now two data paths. One with the data (training data) of the 70% to make the model. This will flow to the input of the model widget. We will use the SVM model here (a classification model). SVM works well even if you have a small number of training samples because it tries to find the best boundary (called a hyper plane) that separates classes with the maximum margin. This makes it less likely to be overfit on small datasets compared to some other models. Overfitting means essentially the model does not generalize and it too custom for the data it was trained on.

Add to the workflow a SVM widget and a Test and Score widget. Set the connector from the Data Sampler to SVM to have the Data Sample – Data (this is the 70% data) and the connector from the Data Sampler to the Test and Score as 'Remaining Data' (click on connectors to do this). Set up this flow EXACTLY as depicted below (the training data goes through the model and then to test and score which takes in the model and the remaining data that it uses to test the model that has not been through the model).

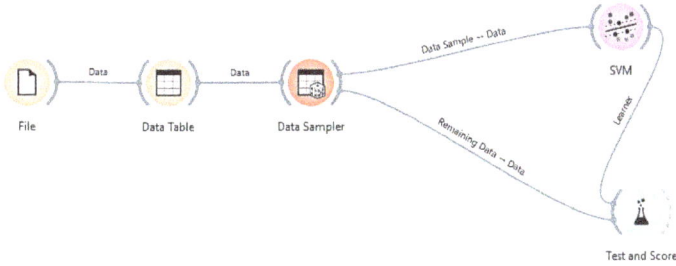

Step 5 Test and Evaluate

Open the Test and Score Widget.Based on this sample the model has an accuracy of 7/9 or 77.8%. This also is the value in the CA metric of the test and score (which is classification accuracy).Note because this is based on sampling the results here will vary (you may not get the same 'answer' as shown).

Next add a Confusion matrix to the end of the workflow and open this. Note because this is based on sampling the results here will vary. What this particular result shows is that 7 of the 9 test data points were accurately predicted by the model and two (in red on the confusion matrix) of them were misclassified. One misclassified value predicted churn when there was no actual and the other misclassification predicted no churn when there was no churn.

Test and Score   Confusion Matrix

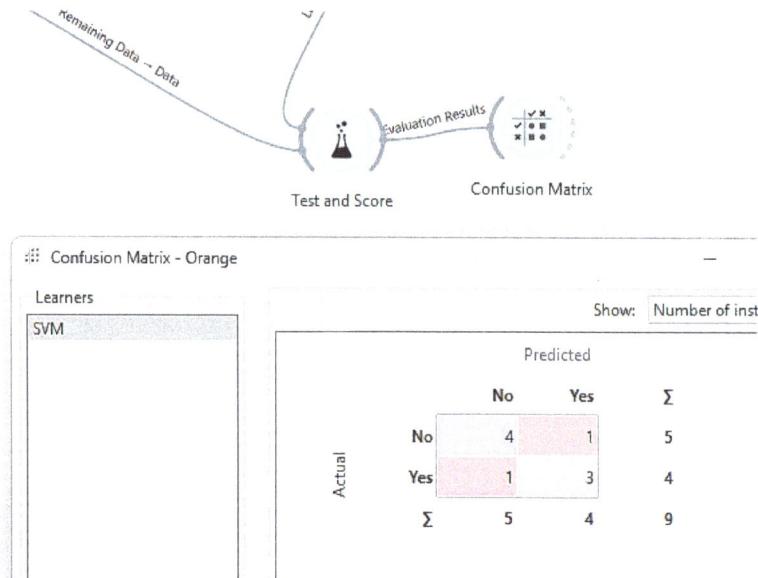

The resulting model of this SVM classification is a reasonable model that helps predict whether customers will churn based on their data. This prediction is useful for businesses to identify at-risk customers and take steps to keep them. Ultimately, the goal is to make better decisions and improve customer retention.

14.2   Wrap-Up

In this lab, you learned how to build and evaluate a classification model. You started by loading the dataset and setting the target variable. Then, you split the data into training and test sets to ensure a fair evaluation of the model's performance on unseen data. Using the SVM algorithm, you trained a model to distinguish between two outcomes. Finally, you assessed the model's accuracy with a confusion matrix. This process highlights how classification models can help businesses to evaluate new data to improve business processes and outcomes.

14.3   Exercises

Classification Analysis

Dataset 1: Email Spam Detection

This dataset (email_spam.csv) simulates email messages labeled as Spam or Not Spam, with features like EmailLength, NumLinks, and NumUppercase-Words.

1. Open the dataset email_spam.csv using the File widget. What do the first 6 rows look like? Use the Data Table widget to inspect.

2. Determine the class distribution. What percentage of emails are labeled as Spam vs Not Spam? Use the Distributions widget and select Spam.

3. Analyze the average number of links. What is the average NumLinks in emails labeled Spam versus Not Spam? Use the Box Plot widget, set Group By = Spam, and select NumLinks.

4. Split the dataset into training and test sets. Use the Data Sampler widget to randomly select 75% for training. How many rows are in the training and testing sets?

5. Train a Decision Tree model. Use the training data as input to a Tree widget. Use Test & Score to test the model on the 25% test set. What is the model's accuracy, and what does the confusion matrix show?

Dataset 2: Bank Loan Default Prediction

This dataset (bank_loan.csv) simulates customer information and whether they defaulted on a bank loan.

6. Open bank_loan.csv using the File widget. What are the first 5 rows of data? Use the Data Table widget. What types of features are present? Check using the Select Columns widget.

7. Compare average income. What is the average Income for customers who defaulted vs those who did not? Use the Box Plot widget, group by Defaulted, and select Income.

8. Compare loan amounts. Create a boxplot comparing LoanAmount for Defaulted = Yes vs No. What differences do you see?

9. Train a logistic regression model. Use Select Columns to keep Age, Income, and LoanAmount as features. Use the Logistic Regression widget to train the model. Use Test & Score to evaluate performance on the test set. What is the accuracy and AUC? What do the coefficients of the model show?

10. Make a prediction for a new customer. Age = 50, Income = 65000, LoanAmount = 140000 Create a one-row input file with these values and use the Predict widget to estimate the probability of default. What is the result?

Lab 15

Sentiment Analysis

Sentiment analysis is a way for computers to understand and classify the emotions or opinions expressed in text. Essentially words are encoded numerically and mathematically matched (either with rules or machine learning) to associated feelings or sentiments (positive, negative, neutral).

Sentiment analysis is now very commonly used to gauge public reactions in social media or customer reviews. Sentiment analysis is valuable in helping businesses figure out if the overall mood is positive, negative, or neutral. Trends can be monitored, and sentiment shifts from positive to negative may of concern.

There are two main approaches to sentiment analysis. One is machine learning based and very similar to classification analysis. The second method is rule-based which literally uses a rule book or lexicon. This is essentially a list of words that are mapped to sentiment (for example 'awful' maps to negative sentiment). Words like "amazing" get high positive scores, while words like "terrible" receive negative ones. When analyzing a sentence, the system sums these scores to determine the overall sentiment.

This lab does rule-based sentiment analysis.

15.1 Lesson Steps

Step 1: Load Data

(Note be sure the Text Mining add on is installed in Orange and if not install this first. This feature is not part of the base installation of Orange and needs to be installed to do work with text data).

153

Open a new Orange workflow. Add a Create Corpus widget.

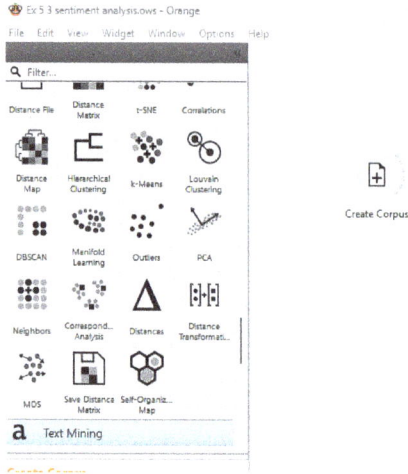

Open the Create Corpus widget and type in the five mini documents shown (you need to push the + sign on the bottom to add documents 4 and 5 as only 3 blank documents are shown by default).

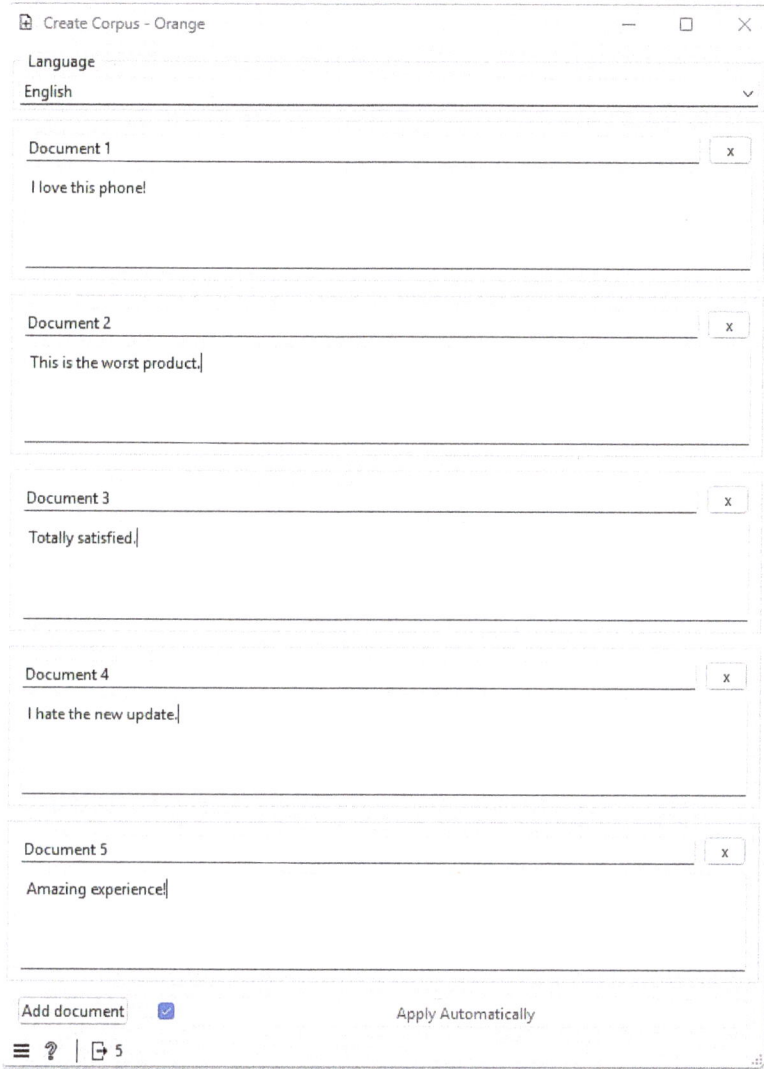

Connect a Corpus Viewer widget and open to assure the documents are correctly entered.

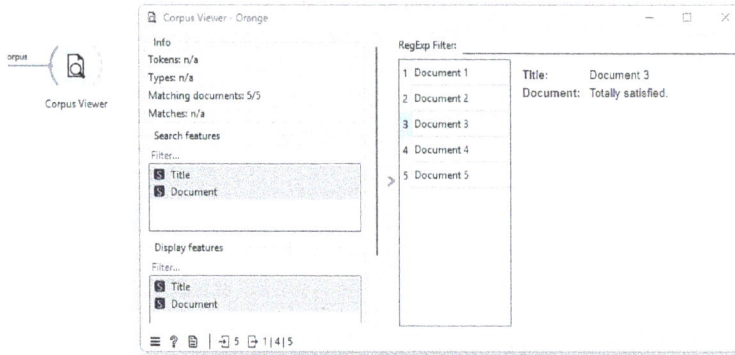

Step 2: Preprocess the Text

All text-based analytics need to go through preprocessing of the text before further analysis. Typically, this involves at a minimum tokenization, making everything lowercase and removing 'stop' words that add little meaning to the analysis.

Add a Preprocess Text widget from the Text Mining menu and connect it to the Create Corpus widget. Open the Preprocessed Text widget and set it as depicted below.

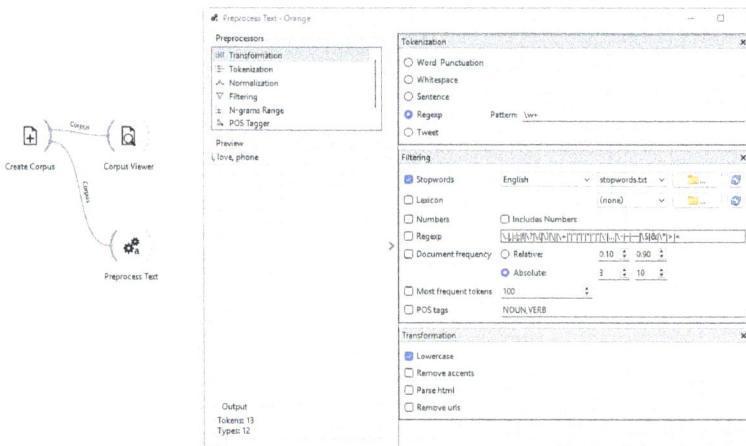

What this will do is tokenize the text, filter for stopwords, and make all the text lowercase. These are common steps in preparing language text for further analysis. Tokenizing the text means breaking the sentence into smaller parts, usually individual words or phrases. For example, the sentence "I love this product" would be split into the tokens: "I", "love", "this", and "product." This makes it easier for the computer to examine each word separately.

Filtering for stopwords removes very common words that usually don't carry much meaning on their own, such as "the," "is," "and," or "in." These words appear often in language but don't help much when determining sentiment or meaning, so removing them helps the analysis focus on more important words.

Making all the text lowercase is done so the computer treats words like "Happy" and "happy" as the same word. Computers are case-sensitive by default, so converting everything to lowercase ensures consistency and avoids counting the same word as different just because of capitalization.

Together, these steps clean and standardize the text, making it easier and more accurate for a sentiment analysis program to work with the data.

Connect a second Corpus viewer to the Preprocess Text widget to view what the preprocessing has done. Make sure the checkbox in the bottom left corner 'Show Tokens and Tags' is checked off (or you can't see the preprocessor results).

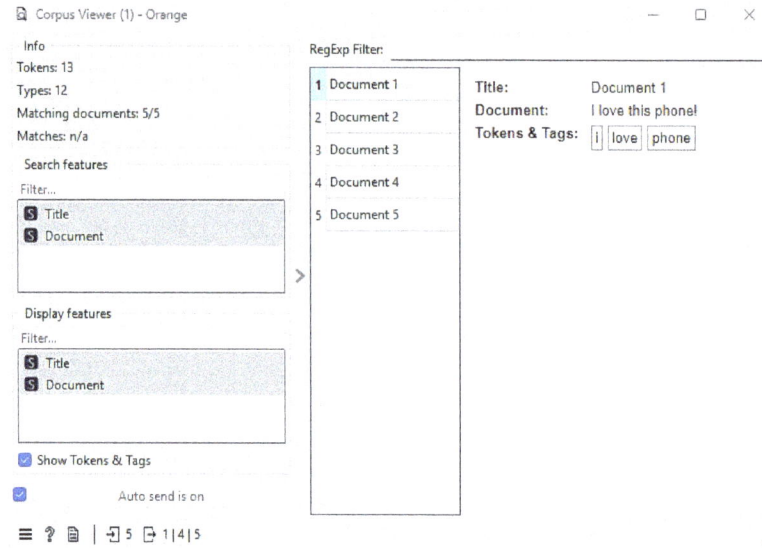

The corpus is now ready for sentiment analysis.

Step 3: Apply Sentiment Analysis

Add a sentiment analysis widget to the workflow. Connect this to the prepro-cess text widget and open it. Select the VADER method.

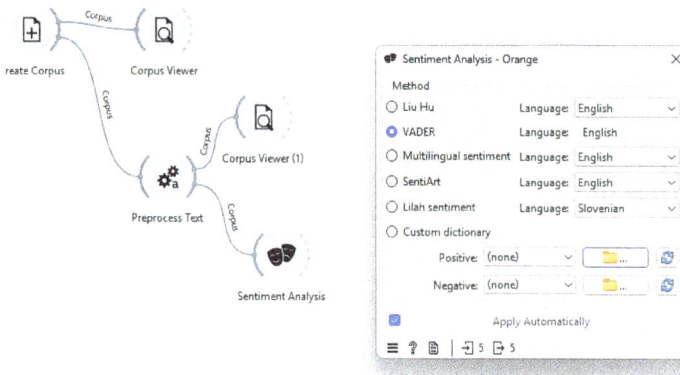

The VADER (Valence Aware Dictionary and sEntiment Reasoner) method is a rule-based sentiment analysis specially designed for analyzing sentiment in social media and short text. It uses a dictionary (aka lexicon or rules) of words with sentiment scores. It includes rules to handle things like capitalization, punctuation, degree modifiers (e.g., "very good"). It is even able to work with emojis and slang. VADER returns a score for positive, negative, neutral, and a compound score that summarizes the overall sentiment of the text.

Step 4: View and analyze results

As discussed above VADER produces scores for sentiment – positive, negative, neutral and compound. Add a Data Table widget to the Sentiment Analysis widget and open it. It will show the scores for the documents in the corpus.

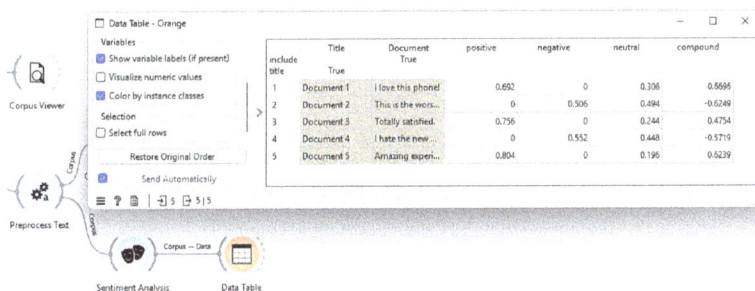

Compound scores - that reflect overall sentiment - are the most important metric in VADER sentiment analysis. If the compound score is greater than 0.05, the sentiment is considered positive. If it is less than –0.05, the sentiment is negative. A score between –0.05 and 0.05 is interpreted as neutral.

The sentence "This is the worst product." is classified as negative by Orange's rule-based Sentiment Analysis (using VADER). The word "worst" carries strong negative weight, while the rest of the words ("This," "is," "product") are neutral. VADER assigns a compound score of –0.6249, meaning clearly negative sentiment. No positive words are detected, and about 50.6% of the content is judged as negative. Since this uses a lexicon-based method (no training), the result depends entirely on the presence of predefined negative words like "worst."

Step 5: Graphically analyze scores

Here the data is small, so the data table view of the output is manageable. However, the scores can also conveniently be viewed using graphical means. One way to do this is with a heatmap. A heat map visually displays sentiment scores for each document using colors, where stronger colors represent higher or lower values. It helps quickly identify patterns of positive, negative, or neutral sentiment across the dataset.

Add a Heat Map widget to the Data Table widget with the sentiment scores and connect them. Open the heat map to view the scores and annotate it with the document text.

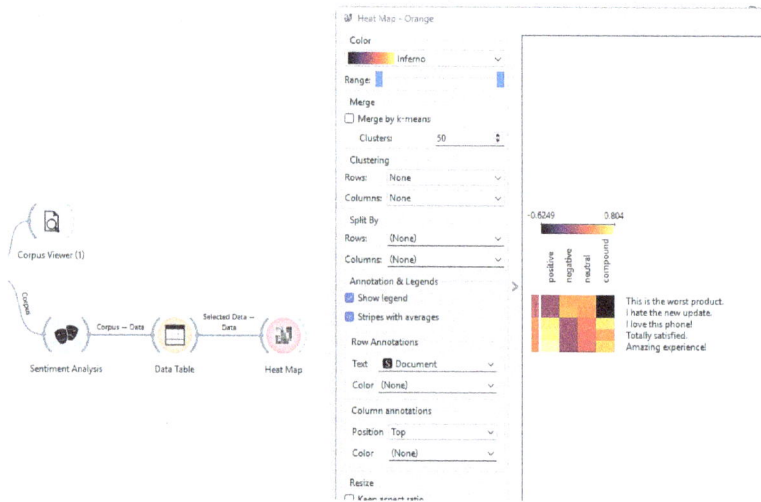

15.2   Wrap-Up

This lab showed how to use Orange to perform sentiment analysis on text data using the rule-based VADER method. You learned how to prepare text by cleaning and standardizing it, then apply sentiment scoring to classify documents as positive, negative, or neutral. Viewing results in both table and heatmap formats helped visualize the sentiment patterns across the documents. Sentiment analysis is an important analytical technique and is becoming very commonplace.

15.3   Exercises

Sentiment Analysis

In this exercise, you'll use two original datasets containing short text snippets to practice rule-based sentiment analysis.

Dataset 1: News Headlines

Simulated news headlines (file news_headlines.csv) showing various tones from positive to negative.

1. Display the first 5 rows of the dataset.
2. After preprocessing (lowercase, tokenize, remove stopwords), list tokens for HeadlineID "H2".
3. What is the compound sentiment score for HeadlineID "H7"?
4. Which headline has the strongest positive sentiment?
5. Create a heatmap of sentiment scores for all headlines. Describe the overall sentiment pattern.

Dataset 2: Restaurant Feedback

Simulated brief feedback comments from customers about a restaurant experience (file restaurant_feedback.csv).

6. Show the structure and first 5 rows of the dataset.
7. After preprocessing, list tokens for FeedbackID "F8".
8. Which feedback comment has the most negative sentiment score?
9. What is the overall sentiment classification for FeedbackID "F6"?
10. Create a bar plot of compound sentiment scores for all feedback comments. Which comment is closest to neutral?

Lab 16

Data Visualization

Visualization in data analytics serves multiple purposes. Formal Data visualization techniques can be taught as a communications subject to non-verbally tell data stories. Study of best practices in data visualization will not be covered here. Also, Orange is NOT the best or optimal tool for this type of data visualization. A tool such as Tableau or the programming graphics available in R are much more optimal for preparing data for professional data visualization purposes.

What Orange does however is provide tools for understanding the types of data you have for the purpose of pre-analysis and very basic plots. Data in Orange can be visualized with charts like histograms to see how values are distributed, box plots to compare groups, or scatter plots to explore relationships between two numeric variables. Categorical data, like whether a patient has heart disease (Yes/No), represent groups or categories can be viewed4d using bar charts or mosaic plots that display counts or relationships between categories.

This lab explores the basic data visualization features available in Orange.

16.1   Lesson Steps

Step 1: Load Data

Open a new workflow and load the data patients.csv.

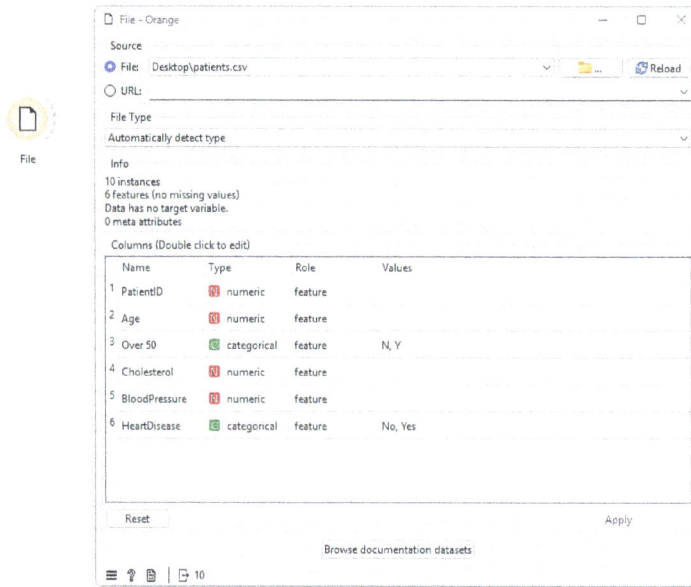

This dataset contains basic health information for ten patients and is designed to help explore the relationship between age, cholesterol, blood pressure, and the presence of heart disease. Each row represents one patient, and the columns capture different types of information, or variables. Some of these variables are numerical, such as age, cholesterol level, and blood pressure, which represent measurable quantities that can be used in calculations and statistical analysis. Others are categorical, such as whether the patient is over 50 years old and whether they have heart disease. These categorical variables sort data into groups, often with values like "Yes" or "No." Understanding the types of variables in a dataset is important because it guides how we summarize, visualize, and analyze the data. This dataset includes a mix of both types, making it useful for learning how to work with different data structures in applied health analysis.

Step 2: Explore Numeric Distributions

To explore how the quantitative variable cholesterol levels are distributed, use a Histogram plot.

To the File widget, add and connect it to a Distribution (aka Histogram) widget from the Visualize menu. Open this and select Cholesterol as the variable to plot. A bin width is the size or interval of each "bin" (or bucket) used in grouping data when creating histograms or frequency distributions. Adjust the bin width to 25.

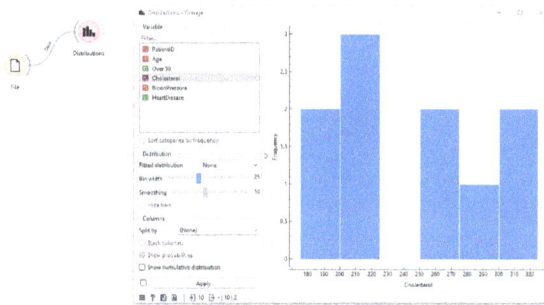

A histogram (the distribution graph) is useful here because it shows how cholesterol values spread across all patients. The overall distribution shows most people in the data fall into a healthy range, if there are any high-risk values, and if the values are clustered or spread out. This helps identify patterns, such as whether high cholesterol is common in this group.

Step 3: Use a Boxplot to Compare

To compare cholesterol levels between patients with and without heart disease, use a Box Plot. Connect the File widget to a Box Plot widget. Set Cholesterol as the variable to analyze and group by HeartDisease.

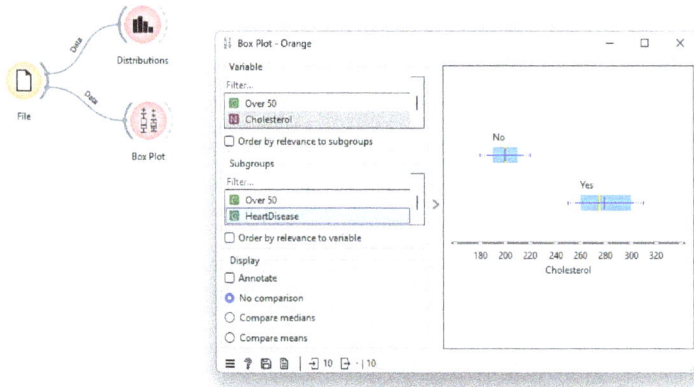

A box plot is ideal here because it displays the median, spread, and outliers of cholesterol values in each group (Yes/No). This allows you to quickly see if patients with heart disease tend to have higher cholesterol, which supports deeper health analysis. The boxplot shows a difference between groups.

Step 4: Use a Scatterplot to View Relations

To check if age is related to blood pressure, add a Scatter Plot widget connected to the File widget. Set the X-axis to Age and the Y-axis to BloodPressure.

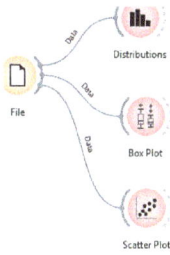

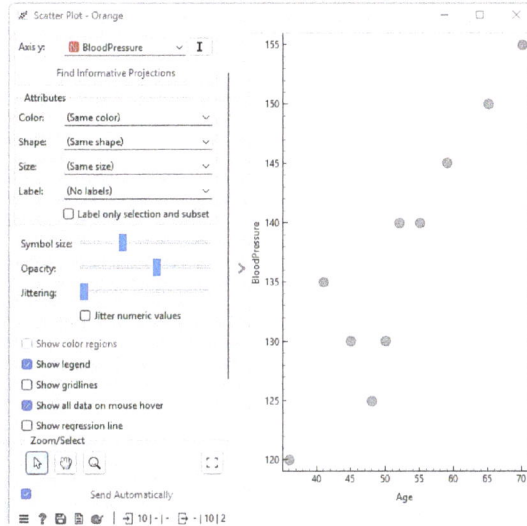

A scatter plot is the best way to explore the relationship between two numerical variables. This visualization helps answer questions like: Do older patients tend to have higher blood pressure? From the graph this appears to be the case.

Orange also in the Scatter plot widget allows color coding by group. Under Attribute – Color select Heart Disease, and the scatterplot is now color coded by the coding in the data for whether the patient has heard disease.

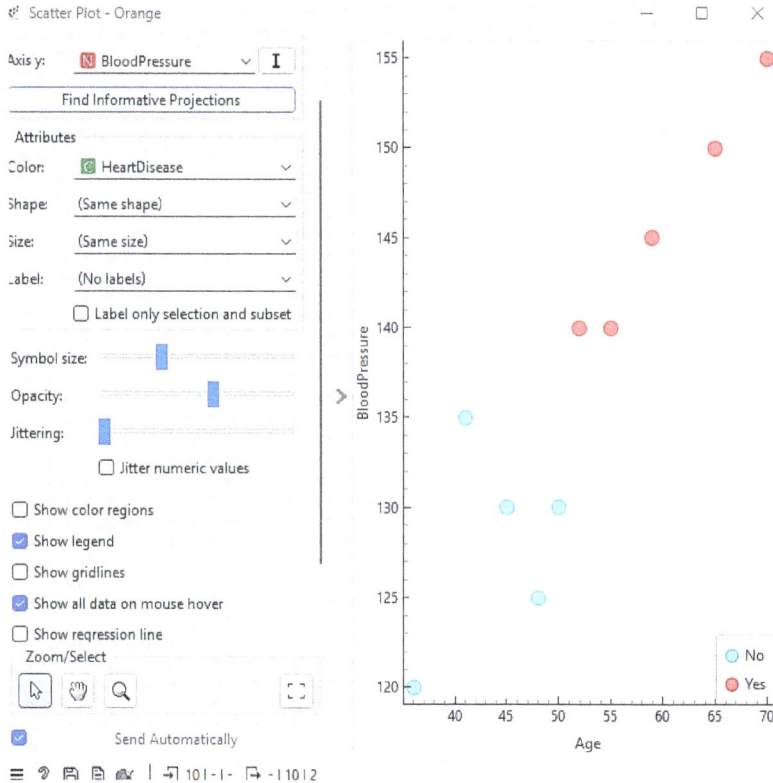

This is very helpful to look at when exploring or presenting a story with the data.

Step 5: Make a Bar Chart

Bar charts are often used to show count totals or other aggregated (summarized) data features. To see how many patients are over 50, we need first to aggregate the data. Connect a Group By widget to the File widget and open it. Set the group by on the left to 'Over 50' and then check the attribute for this to set to count.

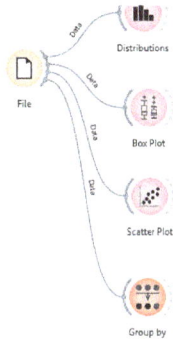

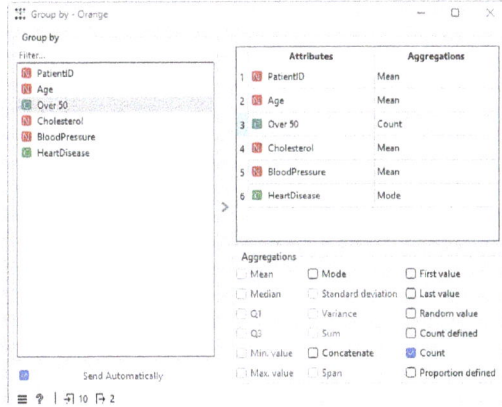

Connect the Group By widget to a Bar graph widget and open this. Set it to display the over 50 data and set it to annotate with the over 50 variables (which will add labels to the axis). Now the graph displays counts of how many patients are over 50 or not.

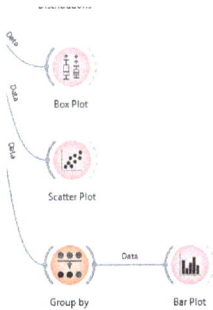

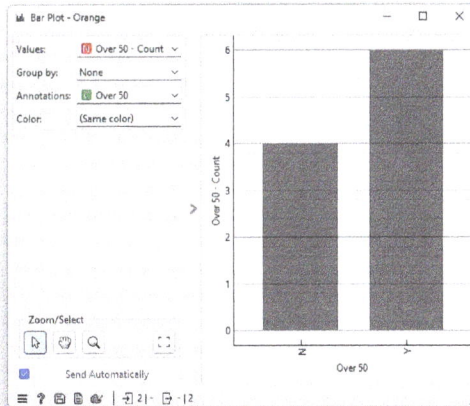

A bar chart is perfect for showing how many cases fall into each category. This gives a quick visual of how common things are in this dataset.

Step 6: Mosaic Chart for Categorical Data

A Mosaic Plot is used to examine the relationship between two categorical variables by dividing a rectangle into proportional sections based on frequencies. In this case, we can use it to explore whether patients over 50 are more likely to have heart disease since these are both categorical variables in our data.

Connect a Mosaic Display widget to the File widget and open it. Set it to look at "Over 50" and "Heart Disease" and color by Heart Disease.

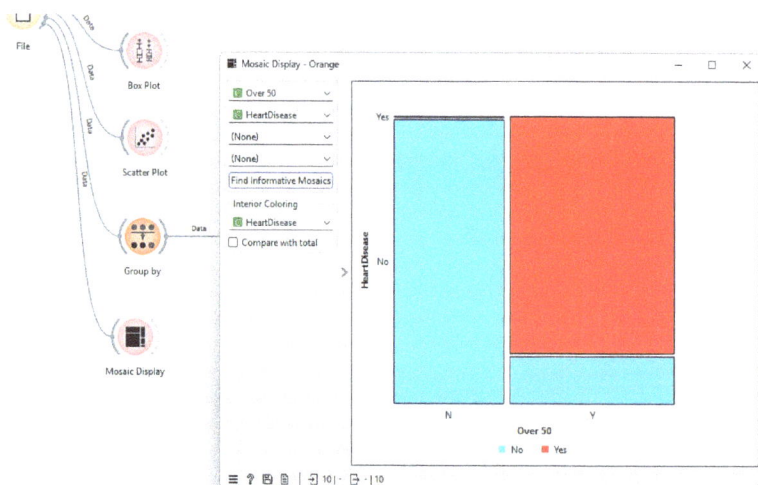

The Mosaic Plot makes it easy to visually compare the proportions of heart disease within each age group. You can quickly spot that a larger percentage of patients over 50 have heart disease compared to those under 50 (which has no patients with heart disease).

16.2 Wrap-Up

This lab introduced ways to visualize different types of data. Orange has features to visualize histograms, box plots, and scatter plots to help understand distributions and relationships. For categorical data, bar charts and mosaic plots reveal counts and associations between groups. These visual tools help turn raw data into clear insights, making patterns easier to spot and supporting better decision-making in analysis.

16.3   Exercises

Visualizing Data

This exercise uses two datasets — retail store sales and movie ratings — to practice different visualization types on numeric and categorical data.

Dataset 1: Retail Store Sales

This dataset (retail_sales.csv) contains daily sales info from 12 retail stores, including total sales, number of customers, and store type.

1. Create a histogram of TotalSales with bin width 2000. What is the most common sales range?
2. Generate a boxplot comparing TotalSales by StoreType. Which store type has the highest median sales?
3. Produce a scatter plot of Customers (X-axis) vs. TotalSales (Y-axis). Describe the relationship.
4. Color code the scatter plot by OpenLate status. Do stores open late tend to have more sales or customers?
5. Create a bar chart of counts of stores that open late vs. not open late. How many stores are open late?

Dataset 2: Movie Ratings

This dataset (movie_ratings.csv) contains 15 movies with genre, critic score, audience score, and whether it won an award.

6. Create a histogram of CriticScore with bin width 10. What is the general distribution?
7. Generate a boxplot comparing AudienceScore by Genre. Which genre has the highest median audience score?
8. Create a scatter plot of CriticScore (X-axis) vs. AudienceScore (Y-axis). Describe the correlation.
9. Produce a bar chart showing counts of movies by AwardWon status. How many movies won awards?
10. Use a mosaic plot to explore the relationship between Genre and AwardWon. Which genre has the highest proportion of award winners?

Lab 17

Bias in Models

In this tutorial, you will explore how machine learning models can exhibit bias—unfair performance differences across groups—when trained on real-world data.

Specifically, you'll examine whether a model trained to predict income level (target: <=50K or >50K) behaves differently for people of different gender (Male, Female). You'll learn how to load and prepare data, build a classification model, evaluate its performance, and compare model accuracy and fairness across subgroups.

This hands-on exercise highlights how bias can appear in seemingly objective algorithms. This is a very important issue to be aware of in the age of AI.

17.1 Lesson Steps

Step 1: Load the Data

Open a new workflow, add a File widget and upload the incomeEquity.csv data.

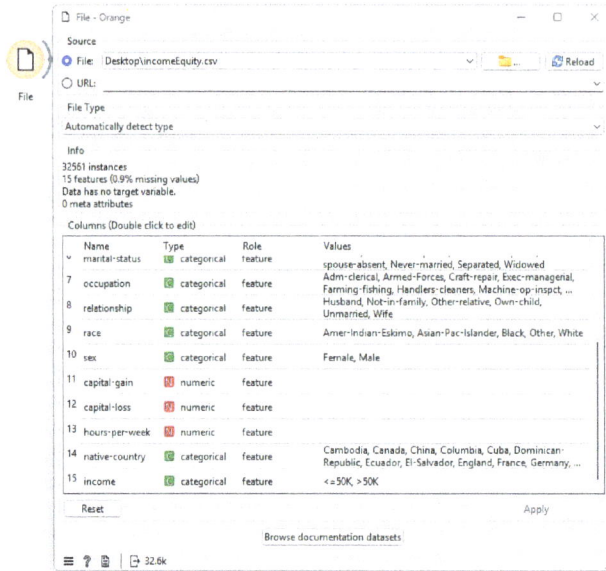

Step 2: Look at Data

Add a data table widget and open it to look over the data.

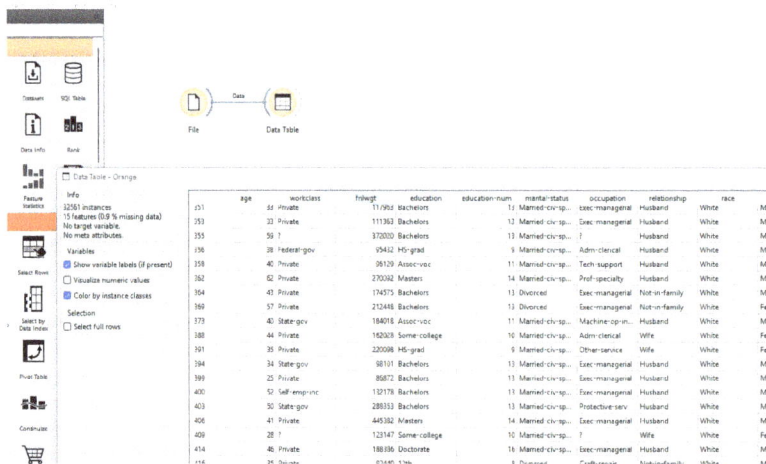

Step 3: Select Features and Target

Connect a select columns widget. Set the target variable to income (this is a binary variable under or over 50K).

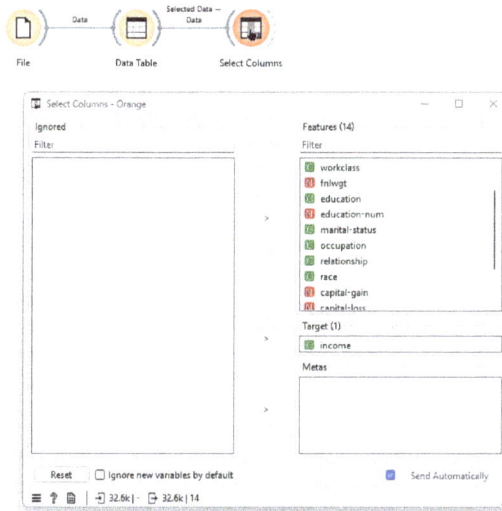

Step 4: Look at income distribution by gender

Add a Distributions widget and connect it to the data table. Set it to look at income and split columns by sex.

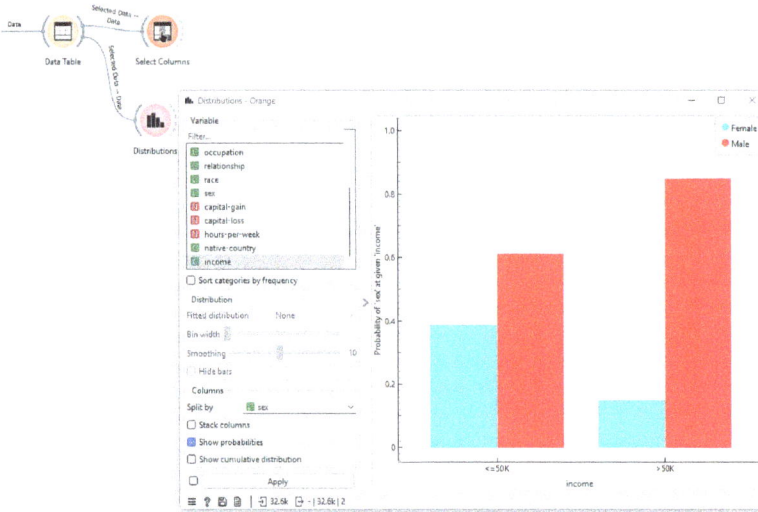

Note that the distribution of > 50 K is predominantly male and that income clearly is not evenly distributed by gender.

Step 5: Make Pooled Model

Next let's do a model of logistic regression with income (binary greater or less than 50K) as our outcome and all features as an input. To set this up in Orange add a Logistic Regression and a Test and Score widget as shown and hook this up to the Select Columns widget as shown.

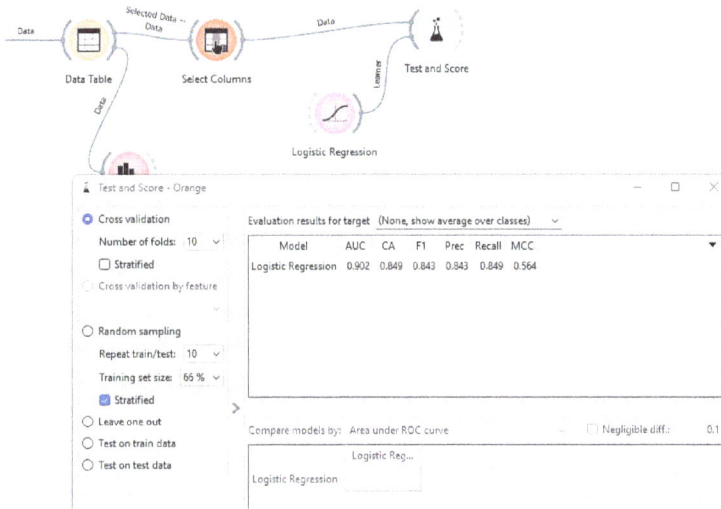

Open the Test and Score widget and set the Cross Validation option to 10-fold as shown. Cross-validation is a way to test how good your model is by checking it on different parts of your data. Instead of training and testing the model just once, the data is split into small parts, and the model is tested several times—each time on a different part. This gives you a more accurate idea of how well the model will work on new data, not just the data it was trained on.

Allow the model to run (this may take a few minutes as it is a large dataset, and the cross validation takes some time to process). Ultimately the results of accuracy metrics are shown. The overall model accuracy is the 'CA' metric which is 0.849. This means that over 85% of the data is correctly classified by the model (given the feature inputs 85% of the time the model correctly classified income as over or under 50k).

Step 6: Make Separated Models

The above accuracy rate is based on all genders. Let's see what happens when we divide the data and run it independently on females and males.

First add connected to the Select Columns widget add a Select rows widget and set it to equal to female. Set up connected to this a Logistic regression widget and a Test and Score widget. Set the test and score widget to 10-fold cross validation and allow the model to run.

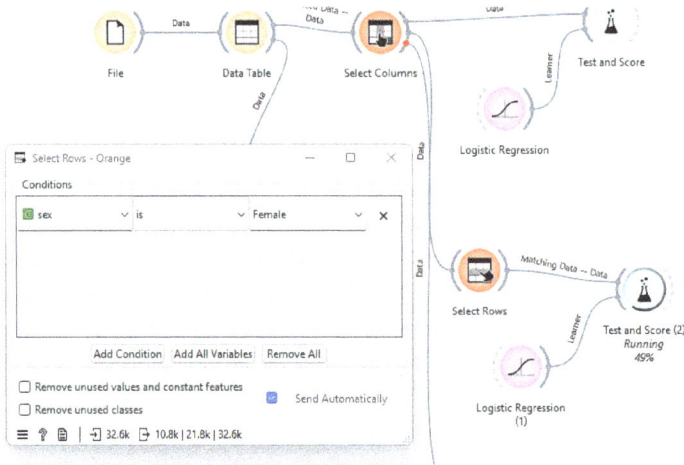

Second add connected to the Select Columns widget add another Select rows widget and set it to equal male. Set up connected to this a Logistic regression widget and a Test and Score widget. Set the test and score widget to 10-fold cross validation and allow the model to run.

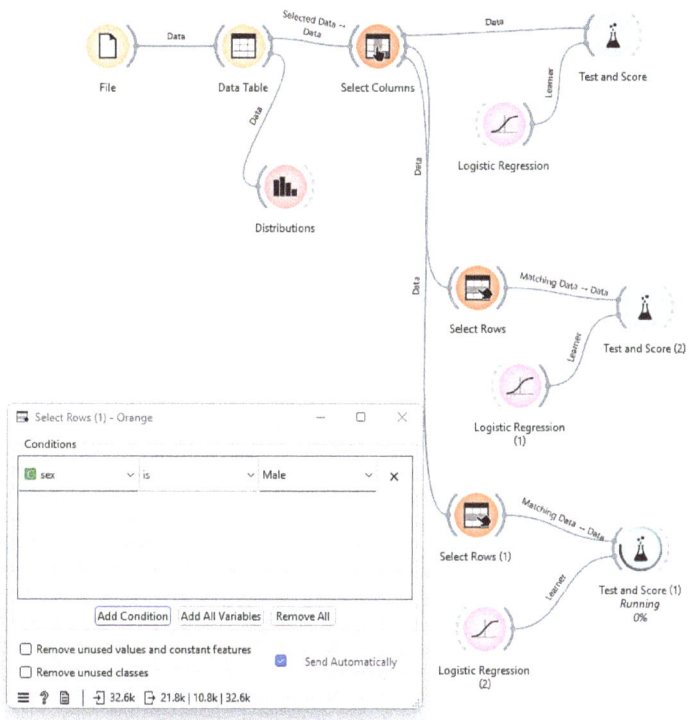

Step 7: Compare Models

From Step 5 the overall model accuracy was roughly 85%. But this was for pooled genders. Open the Test and Score widget for the females after the model has completed.

Open the Test and Score widget for the males after the model has completed. (Note because this is sampling results may slightly vary but overall conclusion should be consistent).

The model accuracy for females is 92.5% whereas for males the model is only 81.3% (look at the CA metric). The model performs with different accuracy for different genders. Examples like this of bias — unfair performance differences across groups – are problematic. Without running models segregated by gender this would not be detected. This example highlights the importance of analyzing model effectiveness across groups and ensuring fairness of models that are implemented.

17.2 Wrap-Up

In this lab, you explored how machine learning models can behave differently across groups, even when trained on the same data. While the overall model seemed accurate, breaking it down revealed a clear gap in performance for different groups. This is the concept of bias in models and in general a bad thing to have.

This kind of difference can have real consequences in practice, especially when algorithms are used to make decisions that affect people's lives—such as lending, hiring, or healthcare access. Just because a model performs well overall doesn't mean it's fair.

Understanding and addressing these disparities is a key step toward building more responsible and equitable data systems.

17.3   Exercises

Bias in Models

This exercise will explore how model performance may differ unfairly across groups. Follow the procedure in lab 7 training classification models, observe how models behave with different groups, and comparing results to determine if the model is unbiased and treats both groups equitably (as measured by its accuracy by group).

Dataset 1: University Admissions

This dataset (univ_admissions.csv) contains 14 university applicants with features about their academic records and demographics. The goal is to predict admission (Admit: Yes/No) and examine if model performance differs by Gender (Male/Female).

1. Load the university admissions data into Orange. How many records and variables are there?

2. Examine the distribution of Admit by Gender using a Distribution or Bar chart widget. Which gender has a higher admission rate?

3. Train a logistic regression model to predict Admit using GPA, SAT, and Extracurricular. What is the overall accuracy (CA) with 10-fold cross-validation?

4. Use a Select Rows widget to filter for Gender = Male. Train and evaluate the model again. What is the accuracy for males?

5. Repeat for Gender = Female. Compare the inaccuracies. Does the model perform differently?

Dataset 2: Online Course Completion

This dataset (course_completion.csv) contains 12 students enrolled in an online course. The goal is to predict whether they completed the course (Complete: Yes/No) and assess bias by AgeGroup (Young, Older).

6. Load the course completion dataset into Orange. How many students completed the course versus those who did not?

7. Visualize StudyHoursPerWeek distribution by Complete status using a Box Plot or Histogram. What trends do you notice?

8. Build a logistic regression model predicting Complete from Study-HoursPerWeek and PreviousExperience. What is the overall model accuracy?

9. Filter data for AgeGroup = Young and train the model again. What accuracy is achieved?

10. Repeat for AgeGroup = Older. How do model accuracies compare? What might this suggest about bias?

www.ingramcontent.com/pod-product-compliance
Lightning Source LLC
Chambersburg PA
CBHW051928190326
41458CB00026B/6444